OTHER BOOKS BY
JULES ARCHER

African Firebrand: Kenyatta of Kenya

Angry Abolitionist: William Lloyd
Garrison

Battlefield President: Dwight D.
Eisenhower

Breaking Barriers: The Feminist
Revolution

China in the Twentieth Century

Chou En-lai

Colossus of Europe: Metternich

Congo

The Dictators

Earthquake!

Epidemic!

The Executive "Success"

The Extremists: Gadflies of American
Society

Famous Young Rebels

Fighting Journalist: Horace Greeley

From Whales to Dinosaurs

Front-Line General: Douglas
MacArthur

Hawks, Doves, and the Eagle

Ho Chi Minh: The Legend of Hanoi

A House Divided: Ulysses S. Grant
and Robert E. Lee

Hunger on Planet Earth

Hurricane!

The Incredible Sixties

Indian Foe, Indian Friend

Jungle Fighters: A G.I. War
Correspondent's Experiences in the
New Guinea Campaign

Laws That Changed America

Legacy of the Desert

Man of Steel: Joseph Stalin

Mao Tse-tung: A Biography

Mexico and the United States

1968: Year of Crisis

The Philippines' Fight for Freedom

The Plot to Seize the White House

Police State

Rage in the Streets: Violence in
America

Red Rebel: Tito of Yugoslavia

Resistance

Revolution in Our Time

Riot! A History of Mob Action in the
United States

The Russians and the Americans

Special Interests: How Lobbyists
Influence Legislation

Strikes, Bombs, and Bullets: Big Bill
Haywood and the I.W.W.

Superspies

They Had a Dream: The Civil Rights
Struggle

They Made a Revolution: 1776

Thorn in Our Flesh: Castro's Cuba

Tornado!

Treason in America: Disloyalty Versus
Dissent

Trotsky: World Revolutionary

Twentieth-Century Caesar: Benito
Mussolini

Uneasy Friendship: France and the
United States

The Unpopular Ones

Washington vs. Main Street

Watergate: America in Crisis

Who's Running Your Life?

World Citizen: Woodrow Wilson

You and the Law

You Can't Do That to Me!

Winners and Losers: How Elections
Work in America

"To Save the Earth"

THE AMERICAN ENVIRONMENTAL MOVEMENT

Jules Archer

VIKING

VIKING
Published by the Penguin Group
Penguin Putnam Inc., 375 Hudson Street, New York, New York 10014, U.S.A.
Penguin Books Ltd, 27 Wrights Lane, London W8 5TZ, England
Penguin Books Australia Ltd, Ringwood, Victoria, Australia
Penguin Books Canada Ltd, 10 Alcorn Avenue, Toronto, Ontario, Canada M4V 3B2
Penguin Books (N.Z.) Ltd, 182-190 Wairau Road, Auckland 10, New Zealand

Penguin Books Ltd, Registered Offices: Harmondsworth, Middlesex, England

First published in 1998 by Viking, a member of Penguin Putnam Inc.

1   3   5   7   9   10   8   6   4   2

LIBRARY OF CONGRESS CATALOGING-IN-PUBLICATION DATA:
Archer, Jules.
To save the earth : the American environmental movement / Jules Archer.
p. cm.
Includes bibliographical references and index.
Summary: Presents a brief history of the environmental movement and accounts of
the work of four environmental activists: John Muir, Rachel Carson,
David McTaggart, and Dave Foreman.
ISBN 0-670-87121-4
1. Environmentalists—United States—Biography—Juvenile
literature. 2. Environmentalism—United States—History—Juvenile
literature. 3. Muir, John, 1838-1914—Juvenile literature.
4. Carson, Rachel, 1907-1964—Juvenile literature. 5. McTaggart,
David Fraser, 1932—Juvenile literature. 6. Foreman, Dave, 1946—
Juvenile literature. [1. Muir, John, 1838-1941. 2. Carson,
Rachel, 1907-1964. 3. McTaggart, David Fraser, 1932-   .
4. Foreman, Dave, 1946-   . 5. Environmentalists. 6. Environmental
protection.] I. Title. II. Series.
GE55.A73 1998 333.7'2'092273 [B]—DC21 97-35373 CIP AC

Printed in U.S.A.
Set in Bodoni Book
Book design by Two Rivers Design

 Printed on recycled paper

To my newest granddaughters,

Zoë Alena Archer and

Nikkita Paige Archer,

and my other grandchildren

in the hope that they will enjoy, cherish,

and preserve the earth they have inherited

· CONTENTS ·

· INTRODUCTION ·

ENVIRONMENTALISTS FIGHT TO HALT the pollution of our air, oceans, lakes, and rivers that endangers our health and the quality of our lives. Among the polluters are irresponsible nations and powerful corporations that place huge profits above preserving the environment and all the life forms dependent upon it.

Among those who have fought heroically to save the earth for us are four extraordinary environmentalists who devoted their lives to achieving that goal.

John Muir's love affair with the wilderness stirred millions of Americans to fight to preserve our beautiful virgin lands. He fostered our national park system, beginning with Yosemite National Park.

Rachel Carson's love of the sea made Americans aware of the need to keep our oceans and tidelands unpolluted. She also initiated a great crusade that eliminated many pesticides, and the dumping of chemical wastes dangerous to humans, wildlife, and sea life.

David McTaggart was outraged by governments that spread death and disease by exploding nuclear bombs in the atmosphere and killed whales and baby seals for profit. He organized environmentalists into Greenpeace to stop those forces of destruction nonviolently. The Greenpeacers risk death by blocking offending nations' ships with their own bodies.

Dave Foreman was frustrated by the failure of the preaching and politics of conservative environmental groups to stop powerful business interests from violating the ecology. He organized Earth First! using "monkeywrenching," hands-on tactics to stop the despoilers and save our forests.

This book highlights the contributions of these four dedicated environmentalists to whom all of us owe an undying debt of gratitude for their courageous struggle to save this one earth we share with each other and our wildlife.

I wish to thank David McTaggart, founder of Greenpeace; Dave Foreman, former leader of Earth First!; and Dan Haifley, leader of Save Our Shores, for granting me interviews and for their cooperation.

I am also indebted for their cooperation to the Library of Congress; Patricia Middleton of the Beinecke Rare Book and Manuscript Library at Yale; Gary Trudeau of *Doonesbury;* Phoebe Adams, Head Librarian, Sierra Club; James Timpert, archivist of the Johns Hopkins University Archives; Norma Craig of the Visuals Center, National Park Service; Nora McCarthy and Elizabeth Sommerville of Greenpeace; Earthsave; Richard Ogar of the Bancroft Library, Berkeley; Mary Suggett of Universal Press Syndicate; the U.S. Environmental Protection Agency; and Shirley A. Briggs, Executive Director Emeritus of the Rachel Carson Council, Inc.

Jules Archer
Scotts Valley, California

To Save the Earth

John Muir.
(Photograph courtesy of William E. Colby Memorial Library, Sierra Club)

John Muir

1 8 3 8 – 1 9 1 4

*"Do Something for Wildness
and Make the Mountains Glad"*

· ONE ·

ASSAULTED BY A RAGING SNOWSTORM that blotted out the vastness of Alaska's Taylor Glacier, mountaineer John Muir plunged ahead with his dog companion, Stickeen. Suddenly he was confronted by a crevasse a thousand feet deep and fifty feet wide. Snow frosted his silken brown hair and beard as his bright blue eyes squinted across the crevasse. To left or right, it looked equally wide and forbidding.

Muir deliberated. He could stop here and try to keep himself from being frozen solid by stamping around all through the fast-falling Arctic night. Or he could attempt to cross the crevasse on a narrow diagonal ice bridge ten feet below.

Muir had skirted numerous crevasses, and had simply leaped over those six feet wide or less. Stickeen had proved a marvelous jumper as well, easily flying across the chasms after him. But trying to cross this one on a fifty-foot-long piece of ice, its top tapered to an edge like a razor-sharp ax head, seemed like a certain invitation to death for both of them.

"Of the many perils encountered in my years of wandering on mountains and glaciers," Muir recalled later, "none seemed so plain and stern and merciless as this."

Ignoring the blinding storm, Muir gripped his ice ax and leaned over the crevasse wall. He carefully notched steps for his feet and holds for his hands. Then, slipping cautiously down into them, one side to the wall, he continued to chop notches down to the sliver bridge. He climbed down and held on firmly while he chipped away at the sharp apex of the bridge to make a level seat eight inches wide.

Carefully transferring his weight from the wall, he straddled the slippery sliver bridge. Now he drew a deep, tense breath. The worst still lay ahead.

Inch by inch he chipped his way across, sliding forward while gripping the mere six- to-eight-inch width of ice between his thighs. He fought an urge to stare down into the steep abyss on either side, into which he would plunge if the storm winds threw him off balance on the slippery ice spine. He fixed his blue eyes only on the sliver bridge.

"To me," he recalled, "the edge of that blue sliver was then all the world."

After an eternity, his hands encountered the opposite crevasse wall. He heaved a hoarse sigh of relief, scarcely able to believe he had forced himself across the chasm. But now he had to cut hand and footholds in the opposite ice wall so he could climb back up to the glacier field.

Exhausted and frozen, he braced himself against the storm winds as he struggled up the last steps to safety. "Never before had I been so long under deadly strain," he wrote. "How I got up that cliff I never could tell. The thing seemed to have been done by someone else."

Heaving himself up weakly onto the surface of the oppo- site glacier field, he lay as though dead for a moment. Then he rose on trembling legs, turned, and urged Stickeen to cross over on the sliver bridge as he had.

"You can do it, boy!" he cried. "Come on, come on!"

But Stickeen only howled in anguish, running back and forth as he futilely sought another way across the huge ice ravine. Then he lay down and moaned. At last, responding to Muir's urging, he slid down the glacier wall, braking with his legs in Muir's notches. Crossing the sliver bridge, Stickeen sprang at the opposite glacier wall. Hooking his paws into Muir's notches, he scrambled up to safety. Then he darted around in excited circles, rolling over in sheer joy.

That treacherous journey in 1881 was neither the first nor the last time that John Muir would risk his life to explore, challenge, enjoy, and lose himself in the wilderness. To Muir, that was the only way to live.

· T W O ·

A NATURE-INTOXICATED WANDERER, John Muir was also something of a genius. He was an inventor, botanist, horticulturist, geologist, mountaineer, glaciologist, Arctic explorer, pioneer of conservation, and father of our national park system.

Born April 21, 1838, in Dunbar, Scotland, east of Edinburgh, John Muir bore an appropriate family name. Muir in Scottish dialect means moor, a rolling expanse of uncultivated land.

"When I was a boy in Scotland," he said, "I was fond of everything that was wild, and all my life I've been growing fonder and fonder of wild places and wild creatures."

Every chance he got, John would race off to explore the fields, woods, and shore near his home, much to his father's displeasure. Daniel Muir was a dour, stern farmer who often whipped John for neglecting farm chores to take off on nature expeditions. John's mother was a quiet, affectionate woman who took interest in John's excited discoveries of new flowers and birds. His grandfather was also a strong influence on the boy, taking him for walks along the ocean and into the woods.

With his brother David, John loved to explore castle ruins in the neighborhood. He would climb their highest peaks and walls with the zest and disregard for danger that later marked his mountaineering. The boys would dare each other to climb down into dungeons beneath the castles, which they named "hell." Once a servant girl scolded John for being naughty and threatened that he would go to hell.

"So what?" he retorted. "If I do, I'll just climb out of it. I know I can because I did!"

John achieved the reputation of being a "cheeky rascal," with a talent for swearing. Corporal punishment was an accepted punishment in John's day, and he received more than his share of whippings at school and at home for fighting. John expressed indignation that "father and teacher should thrash us so industriously for our good, while begrudging us the pleasure of thrashing each other for our own good."

Showing an early love of birds, he would find baby larks in their nest, cage and feed them, and enjoy their company. After a year or two he would release them in the spring, delighting in their flight to freedom.

A momentous event occurred in John's life on February 19, 1849, when he was eleven. He, David, and his sister Sarah were taken by their father aboard a sailing ship to make a new home for the family in America. Once Daniel Muir was established, his wife and other four children would follow.

John's father ended up homesteading in northern Wisconsin. John and David never received any formal schooling in America, but were forced to do heavy farmwork, often from dawn to dusk in freezing weather. John escaped every chance he could to roam in the forests. Their father was a harsh taskmaster who did not hesitate to whip his sons for the slightest infraction of his rules. He was also a religious zealot and compelled them to memorize Bible verses every day.

But John rebelled against religion because of what he saw as hypocrisy in adults who did not practice what they preached. He was especially incensed by their brutal treatment of both the animals and humans they employed. John seethed at the whippings he received at almost every day's end, even when he'd already been worked to exhaustion, and even when his father had no reason to punish him.

"I don't know any wrong you have done this day," his father would say, "but I'll thrash you just the same for I have no doubt you deserve it." As long as John lived, he never forgot or forgave his father's harsh treatment.

At the age of twelve he was set to plowing, although his head barely reached the plow handles. His father also put him to work clearing land, splitting rails into fences and firewood, and chopping out tree stumps. "This and other heavy jobs stopped my growth," John wrote, "and earned for me the title 'Runt of the family.'"

His workday was at least sixteen hours, winter as well as summer. Even when John fell sick, his father would order him into the fields. Once when he came down with pneumonia, he was allowed to recover in bed without medicine or a doctor, then promptly returned to his sweaty labors. "God and hard work," said his father, "are by far the best doctors."

· THREE ·

IN HIS MIDTEENS JOHN ESCAPED the confines of his father's theological views by borrowing books from neighbors. The drabness of his existence fell away when he entered the intoxicating worlds of Shakespeare, Milton, Plutarch, Walter Scott, and other great writers. He had to read the books secretly, though, as his father considered all sectarian books "works of the devil." Daniel Muir declared, "The Bible is the only book human beings can possibly require throughout all the journey from earth to heaven."

But John's mind expanded with the beauty of the fine poetry and worldly thought in his borrowed books. By selling muskrat and squirrel skins, he saved enough to buy his own books of English poetry, mathematics, and grammar. These he studied in stolen moments during mealtimes and after evening family worship. When the family retired, John would often stay up reading in the kitchen by candlelight until ordered to bed.

"If you *will* read," his exasperated father said finally, "get up in the morning and read." So John slept only five hours a night, awakening at 1:00 A.M. to read away happily until dawn. But when winter came, his father refused to allow him to use firewood to keep warm while reading. John, by this time used to 1:00 A.M. risings, decided to put the midnight hours to another use—inventing things.

In the basement workshop he made his own tools out of waste scraps of wood, steel, and wire. With these and his lively imagination, he invented a whole series of functional gadgets to make his farmwork easier, carving their intricate parts with patient precision and skill.

Damming a small stream, he made falling water turn a wooden waterwheel he invented to operate a saw that cut firewood. He had never seen the insides of a clock or watch, yet he invented a grandfather clock that struck the hour in the Muir parlor. Another of his clocks operated his "early rising machine." At his desired time of awakening, the clock would tip John to his feet by tilting his bed, which was balanced on a fulcrum. He made similar devices to start fires in the fireplace and light lamps automatically. John's father didn't approve of this enterprise any more than of John's books, and called his inventions "nonsensical things" and a waste of time.

Daniel Muir kept his son hard at work. When he bought a new farm at Hickory Hill, he compelled John to dig its well. Striking sandstone ten feet down, John had to spend months in the cramped three-foot-wide well digging the rocks out with a hammer and chisel. When the well reached eighty feet deep, John was almost suffocated by carbonic acid gas. Crying for help, he collapsed in a lowered wooden bucket and was hauled to the surface unconscious.

As soon as the gas had cleared, John was sent back into

the well. Finally, at ninety feet, he struck water. The experience left him with a permanent throat irritation.

"Father never spent an hour in that well," he noted sourly.

Another close call occurred when John panicked while swimming in Fountain Lake, almost drowning. Disgusted with himself, he rowed out to the middle of the lake and dove in headfirst—his first dive. He swam all the way down to touch the lake bottom before surfacing. "Take that!" he shouted defiantly at his body. Then he repeated his act four times before he had punished himself enough.

By the time he was twenty-two, John felt that he no longer had to obey his father. He'd had enough of Daniel Muir's tyranny and decided to leave home to work on his own. Planning to display his best inventions at the Madison State Fair, he asked his father if he could count on a little money from home if he needed some.

"No," snapped Daniel Muir. "Depend entirely on yourself."

So John Muir set out to test his luck in the world with just the fifteen dollars that he had managed to earn and save.

"I am now adrift on this big sinny world," he wrote in a letter home, "and I don't know how I feel." The figure he presented stamped him unmistakably as a farm rustic—rough homespun clothes, beard and hair long and scraggly.

At the fair he exhibited two of his woodcrafted clocks and "early rising machines." They attracted considerable attention, admiration, and newspaper coverage. He was given a prize of ten dollars for ingenuity and a certificate of merit. "It was considered wonderful," Muir wrote, "that a boy on a farm had been able to invent and make such things, and almost every spectator foretold good fortune."

An inventor at the fair offered Muir a place in his foundry

and machine shop in Prairie du Chien. Muir found the work dull, however, and quit after three months. He now decided to advance his education by entering the University of Wisconsin at Madison, despite never having been to high school.

To earn his tuition, he made and sold some of his inventions and took a series of odd jobs. "I was desperately hungry and thirsty for knowledge," he recalled, "and willing to endure anything to get it." That included living on a diet of bread and molasses, graham flour mush, and an occasional potato.

Muir's account of his self-education impressed the dean, who admitted him first to a preparatory course, then as a freshman. He was fascinated by the geology and chemistry courses taught by Dr. Ezra Carr, who hired him to do chores and to babysit at the Carr home.

Carr's wife, Jeanne, became a powerful influence in Muir's life. A botanist and nature-lover, she recognized in the young man a kindred spirit. Also greatly impressed by his unique inventions, which Muir continued to produce in his dormitory, she advised and encouraged him as a mentor. Through her and the extensive Carr library placed at his disposal, Muir was introduced to the works of such famous contemporaries as naturalist Louis Agassiz and the writers Henry David Thoreau and Ralph Waldo Emerson.

Under Jeanne Carr's tutelage he also shed his rustic appearance, trimming his beard and mustache and taming his wild hair. With a respectable appearance he got a job as a district schoolteacher. One of his fire-lighting devices, operated by a clock timer, had the schoolhouse warm before the pupils arrived.

During the summers Muir earned enough working harvests to see him through the rest of the university year. He never ceased inventing things, and his cluttered dorm room became a showplace to which professors took visitors. Muir took only those courses which interested him. Ignoring others needed to graduate, he left after four years without a degree.

"But I was only leaving one University for another," he explained later, "the Wisconsin University for the University of the Wilderness."

· FOUR ·

MUIR WAS NOT DRAFTED FOR THE Civil War, so he wandered north into Canada, taking odd jobs to support himself while he collected botanical specimens. More important than work was the freedom to wander and study the earth and its plants, and to open his mind and soul to what nature had to teach.

Once in a swamp at sundown, feeling lonely and wondering where to spend the night, he came upon a single rare orchid in bloom. "I never before saw a plant so full of life, so perfectly spiritual," he wrote in his journal. He sat down beside the orchid to admire it. Its lonely isolation reminded him of his own, and its beauty made him weep for joy. He remembered this as one of the two great meetings in his life. (The other would come later, when he met Ralph Waldo Emerson.)

He returned to the United States in 1866. In Indianapolis he went to work for Osgood, Smith & Company, the nation's biggest manufacturer of carriage parts. He immediately set about inventing all kinds of labor-saving devices and machinery improvements. The delighted owners quickly raised his salary from ten dollars to twenty-five dollars a week and offered to make him a future partner.

But Muir told them he was only staying "just long enough to earn a few hundred dollars. Then I am going on with my studies in the woods. . . . I like the inventive work . . . but Nature's attractions are stronger, and I must soon get away."

His departure was hastened by a machinery accident that

almost blinded him. But his eye slowly mended. He wrote, "I bade adieu to all my mechanical inventions, determined to devote the rest of my life to the study of the inventions of God."

Still ailing, he returned home for the summer, collecting botanical specimens along the way. His father was not pleased to see John, accusing him of "walking in the paths of the Devil." Daniel Muir added, "I wish you may be loving your God much more than inventing machines."

"I'll tell you this, father," John retorted hotly. "I've been spending my time a lot nearer the Almighty than you have!"

On the day he left, his father asked, "My son, have you not forgotten something?"

"What have I forgotten, Father?"

"Have you not forgotten to pay for your board and lodging?"

Incredulous, John handed him a gold piece. "You may be very sure," he said, "it will be a long time before I come again."

It was a very long time. Daniel Muir did not see his son again until he was on his deathbed. By then, any semblance of the "God-fearing" religion Daniel had tried to inculcate into his son was gone. Far from seeing the world as evil, to be redeemed only through Christian gloom, the Bible, and prayer, John Muir saw the world as God's beautiful gift to man, to be enjoyed by living outdoors in nature as much as possible.

Pondering his next destination in 1867, John read descriptions of California's Yosemite Valley. He was enthralled by accounts of its magnificent cliffs and waterfalls. However, since he lacked the funds to travel that far west, he decided instead on a one-thousand-mile nature walk to the Gulf of Mexico.

While Muir often slept out under the stars, on cold or rainy nights he sometimes sought lodging and bread at private homes. Since his travels left him looking very much like a tramp, doors were frequently slammed in his face.

Once a couple hesitated when Muir introduced himself as a wandering botanist. But when he enthusiastically described his botanical findings in their neighborhood, they welcomed him to dinner and a room. "All doubts as to my being a decent man vanished," he recalled, "and they both said they wouldn't for anything have turned me away."

· FIVE ·

THE MORE JOHN SAW OF THE American wilderness and its seemingly endless variety of plant life, the more convinced he grew that the conventional religious views of life were wrong. He came to believe that God was nothing less than nature in all its wonderful manifestations, and that people were nothing more than one of God's many creatures.

"The world, we are told, was especially for man," he wrote, "a presumption that is totally unsupported by facts." He challenged the belief system that considered animals to be on earth in order to serve people: sheep to provide their clothing, horses to pull their wagons, cows to provide their milk and meat. He especially scorned the notion that people were ordained by God to kill these creatures whenever they saw fit. Hunting, a sport he had pursued in his youth, he now called "murder business."

To avoid being robbed at night by marauders, Muir often slept in cemeteries, confident that superstition would keep others away. But he contracted malaria from sleeping in the open and collapsed while working in a sawmill. For two months he lay desperately ill and delirious.

Recovering, he borrowed money from his brother David and continued his travels, sailing to Cuba. Then he went on to

New York City, a place that completely bewildered him with its "vast throngs of people, the noise of the streets, and the immense size of the buildings."

Leaving New York in March 1868, he traveled to California in steerage on a sailing ship crowded with emigrants. While on board, he became friends with a Cockney named Chilwell, who agreed to accompany him to the Yosemite of his dreams. When they landed in San Francisco, Muir found himself as lost and oppressed in this big city as he had been in New York.

He asked a passerby for the quickest way out of town.

"Where do you want to go?" the San Franciscan asked.

"Anywhere that's wild," John replied.

He and Chilwell were directed south through the Santa Clara Valley, where John was thrilled to find masses of beautiful spring flowers. After a few weeks they forged on, despite warnings of deep snow and bears, until they finally reached Yosemite Valley. John was overwhelmed by the awesome grandeur of the snow-topped Sierra Nevada mountains.

"A landscape was displayed," he wrote later, "that after all my wanderings still appears as the most beautiful I have ever beheld."

After more wilderness explorations by the two wanderers, during which John made sketches of the scenery and collected plants, he found work harvesting crops, breaking horses, running a river ferry and sheep-shearing. He again took up his correspondence with Jeanne Carr, who offered him unflagging support for his love of nature. In her letters she also guided his reading, opening up new realms of music, art, philosophy, and landscape gardening for him. "You do not know how we hold you in our memories as one apart from all other students," she wrote, "in your power of insight into Nature, and the simplicity of your love for her."

In February 1869, Muir took a job supervising sheep-herding for rancher Pat Delaney. After a spring and summer of this work, he developed a lifelong enmity to sheep ranching. He considered his beloved plants and flowers far more worthy of preservation than the "hoofed locusts" who destroyed valley and mountain vegetation wherever they were pastured.

At this time of his life, Muir was so absorbed in the glories of the mountains that he ignored most conventions of dressing and dining. He usually appeared in tattered trousers and ragged, soiled, buttonless shirts decorated with a wildflower. In winter he added a Scottish cap and long coat to the unique ensemble. His staple diet—when he remembered to eat at all—was oatmeal and hard bread. Despite his lack of fruit, vegetables, and protein, he remained lean, hard-muscled, and energetic. "Just bread and water and delightful toil is all I need," he claimed.

During his weeks of sheep-herding in Yosemite's high country, Muir studied not only the area's wildlife, but also its topography. What had smoothed the mountain domes and valley floor of the Sierras? What accounted for the puzzling presence of huge boulders in the valley? His imagination roamed back to prehistoric times, and suddenly the answer dawned on him. Yosemite and the Sierras, he reasoned, had once been covered by a huge glacier flowing from the north, "grinding down the general mass of mountains" and carrying boulders with them.

Muir discovered living glaciers in Yosemite, still inching slowly downhill, and measured their movements over months. These studies required him to climb to dangerous perches on the canyon rim. If granite flakes beneath his feet had given way, he would have plunged over three thousand feet to his death. But Muir was too affected by the view to worry about the danger. "After withdrawing from such places, excited with the view I had got," Muir wrote, "I would say to myself, 'Now

John Muir at Yosemite.
(Photograph courtesy of William E. Colby Memorial Library, Sierra Club)

don't go out on the verge again.' But in the face of Yosemite scenery cautious remonstrance is vain; under its spell one's body seems to go where it likes with a will over which we seem to have scarce any control."

Muir's glacier theory clashed with the opinion of Joseph D. Whitney, California's state geologist. In Whitney's 1868 *Yosemite Guide-Book*, Whitney insisted that the Valley floor had simply dropped out of the mountains during an earthquake.

But Muir found more evidence for his theory when, in 1871, he undertook the tremendous task of exploring every canyon and peak in the Yosemite region, including all its living glaciers. He published his findings in his first article, called "Yosemite Glaciers," which appeared on December fifth in Horace Greeley's *New York Tribune*.

Years later, when the article was reprinted in *Silliman's Journal*, a respected scientific magazine, Whitney angrily attacked it as utter nonsense. He was dismayed when scientific authorities corroborated Muir's findings.

When Muir had to return from the mountains to the Delaney ranch, he grew impatient to get back to the mountains as soon as possible. "I know that looking from the business standpoint you now occupy," he wrote his brother David, "you will say that I am silly and imprudent, and that I value my time at too cheap a rate . . . but I am bewitched, enchanted and must go."

He confided to his journal, "I am hopelessly and forever a mountaineer."

· S I X ·

TEAMING WITH HARRY RANDALL, a young ranch hand, for the company he sometimes desired, Muir set off once more for Yosemite Valley. There he contacted James H. Hutchings, owner of the pioneer Hutchings Hotel and the leading guide to the Valley floor. He won jobs for Randall and himself designing, building, and operating a sawmill on Yosemite Creek. Muir took the job only when Hutchings agreed that he himself would not have to chop down a single living tree. There were enough trees uprooted by the Valley's winter storms to make a million feet of lumber.

The two men built themselves a one-room cabin facing Yosemite Falls. "I dug a small ditch," Muir wrote, "and brought a stream into the cabin entering at one end, with just current enough to allow it to sing and warble in low, sweet tones, delightful at night while I lay in bed."

Here he lived for two years. While running the sawmill, he made many climbs into the Sierras, even in winter, plowing through waist-deep snow in below-freezing weather. Returning at night, he would classify the flower specimens, bark, cones, mosses, rocks, ferns, and butterflies he collected. He spent hours reading book after book on plants, insects, birds, and animals.

By 1869 Easterners were flocking west on the new transcontinental railroad and more and more people came to see the Yosemite Valley's grandeur. When Hutchings was unavailable, Muir's services were sought as a guide. His enthusiasm was dampened by the apathy of many visitors when he showed them Yosemite Falls and the great domes. He resented the way they dismissed these magnificent views with such "cheap adjectives as pretty and charming," instead of remaining awestruck by these natural wonders.

Once when he took a visitor to the panoramic view from atop Inspiration Point, the visitor was perplexed to see tears in Muir's eyes. He asked what was wrong.

"Man," Muir sighed, "can you see the glory of the Almighty and remain unmoved?"

"Oh, it's very fine." The visitor shrugged. "But I do not wear my heart upon my sleeve."

"Ah, my dear man, in the face of such a scene as this it's no time to be thinking of where you wear your heart!"

Muir felt differently about visitors sent to him by Jeanne Carr, since these were invariably "kindred minds"—scientists, professors, writers, and artists. He wrote her gratefully, "You have sent me all my best friends."

Muir worried that Yosemite's beauty was in danger of being spoiled by its popularity and by the commercial enterprises that were springing up to cater to the ever-increasing crowds. But he continued to welcome and guide celebrated visitors, convinced that those exposed to the Sierras would be willing to fight to protect them. Reading books about Yosemite, Muir felt, could not compare to the act of experiencing the landscape itself. "Everyone needs beauty as well as bread," he wrote. "Our valley is just gushing, throbbing full of open absorbed beauty."

Muir had two favorite spots where he loved to perch and study the Valley and glaciers. One was the summit of the Dome, a huge rock overlooking the Valley. The other was a mountain ledge called Sunnyside Bench, on which he sometimes slept overnight. On both, time ceased to exist for John Muir, for he was in a landscape "more than halfway to heaven."

· SEVEN ·

NOTABLES COMING TO YOSEMITE seeking a guide increasingly asked for Muir instead of Hutchings, who for six years had been the acknowledged Valley guide. One of these celebrities was Ralph Waldo Emerson, whose essays Muir had read and reread. He had sent Emerson an invitation to "join me in a month's worship with Nature in the high temples of the great Sierra Crown beyond our holy Yosemite. It will cost you nothing save the time and very little of that for you will be mostly in eternity."

Emerson, who had heard of Muir, called upon him at the mill. Muir cherished their meeting as one of the greatest moments of his life. He showed Emerson his nature collections and guided the literary giant and his party on horseback to a sequoia grove. Emerson's companions, however, would not allow the delicate Easterner to risk a rugged camping trip with Muir.

When Emerson returned home, Muir sent him letters begging him to return, along with packages of botanical specimens. Emerson wrote him, "I have everywhere testified to my friends . . . my happiness in finding you—the right man in the right place—in your mountain tabernacle." He invited Muir to meet "the larger world you deserve in Concord."

As Muir's reputation as a guide grew, his relations with Hutchings steadily deteriorated. Hutchings was jealous of Muir's fame and complained that he neglected his duties at the mill. In August 1871 Muir wrote to Jeanne Carr, "I am done with Hutchings." He took a new job as caretaker of Black's Hotel in the Valley, where he was allowed more free time to roam the mountains.

In September he became the first man to descend and explore Tuolumne Canyon, a dangerous climb through forty miles of canyon wall rock. Two years later he guided the first woman to enter it—Jeanne Carr. They slid down snow banks to the canyon bottom. Then, "barefooted and [bare] handed we stuck to the glacier-polished rocks and pulled ourselves up."

When the skies dumped a terrible two-day storm onto the Valley, Muir trudged through it happily, experiencing the play of nature's great forces with exhilaration. One night he was shaken awake by a rumbling earthquake. Mastering his fear, he raced out of his cabin to view the shaking mountains as the earth twisted and jerked under his feet. As he fought to keep his balance he heard a tremendous roar. Eagle Rock, high on the south wall of the Valley, sent thousands of boulders and rocks crashing down.

"A noble earthquake, a noble earthquake!" he cried in delight.

Joining a petrified group of Valley residents, Muir laughed, "Come, cheer up! Smile a little and clap your hands. Mother Earth is only trotting us on her knee to amuse us and make us good!"

The others shrank from him as though from a madman.

Muir continually made trips through the summit region, often guiding artists sent to him by Jeanne Carr, who now lived in San Francisco with her husband. He would leave them sketching some beautiful vista while he climbed farther on his own explorations. Once, making his first ascent of Mount Ritter, he found himself stuck halfway up a sheer face, clinging to the rock wall with no further handholds visible.

"Suddenly my danger broke upon me," he related. "Faith and hope failed. . . . Cold sweat broke out. . . . I was alone, cut off from all affinity. Would I fall to the glacier below?"

Paralyzed for a while, he summoned all his mountaineering experience and managed to crawl up the cliff face by clinging to every narrow rift or crack he could find. "Shortly after noon I leaped with wild freedom into the sunlight upon the highest crag of the summit."

Such narrow escapes never deterred him from continuing to risk his neck on challenging, dangerous canyon climbs.

· EIGHT ·

IN SEPTEMBER 1873, MUIR left Yosemite for Oakland to write articles based on his journals. Though the city made Muir ill at ease, it was here that he had access to the reference books and editors he needed. Writing did not come easily to Muir, who despaired of ever finding words that would do justice to the natural wonders he had witnessed. For ten months he labored strenuously over ten articles, most of which would appear in the *Overland Monthly.*

"I care to live only to entice people to look at Nature's loveliness," he wrote in a letter to Jeanne Carr.

Muir was deeply upset whenever he witnessed any new commercial encroachment upon Yosemite by stockmen and lumbermen. "The plow is busy among its gardens," he wrote in 1874, "the axe among its groves, and the whole valley wears a weary, dusty aspect." He urged nature-lovers to "visit the valley at once, while it remains in primeval order."

He studded his articles with pleas for forest protection by the federal government. In 1872 Congress had established Yellowstone National Park as the first protected wilderness in the United States. Muir hoped and worked for the day that his beloved Yosemite would also be taken out of state hands, where it could be easily exploited, and made a national park.

But he was fighting for conservation at a time when people had no regard for the importance of nature because "the world was made for man." Muir believed the opposite. He wanted humanity excluded from nature except as a reverent observer obligated to preserve natural beauty.

After his exhausting writing binge in Oakland, he found it necessary to flee again to Yosemite in September 1874 to restore his spirit. Soon afterward he also began to explore other mountain regions of California.

While exploring the Yuba River Valley, he was caught in a fierce windstorm that sent trees crashing around him and branches flying around his head. Climbing to the summit of a high ridge, he shinned up a one-hundred-foot Douglas spruce to the topmost branch. Swaying violently in the roaring winds, he studied the effects of the storm on the valley. He closed his eyes to listen to and enjoy "the music of the storm."

"I was . . . free to take the wind into my pulses," he wrote, "and enjoy the excited forest from my superb outlook." He did not descend from his dangerous perch until the storm died down.

· **NINE** ·

FROM 1875 TO 1880 MUIR SPENT his summers in the mountains he loved, and his winters in San Francisco writing about them. He explored not only Yosemite and other California regions, but also wildernesses in Utah, Nevada, and Alaska.

The more he wandered, the more incensed he became at the destruction he saw caused by loggers and insatiable herds of sheep, and at the way state legislators bowed to lumber and ranching interests who donated heavily to their election campaigns. In all his writings and speeches, he tried to stir a demand for conservation, urging Americans to view and cherish nature's beauty. He also continued to promote federal control of state forests, particularly Yosemite Valley and the Kings Canyon-Sequoia area.

In the summer of 1878, Muir was invited to join a coast and geodetic survey party under Captain A. F. Rodgers in the highlands of Nevada. As they crossed the Nevada desert, two inexperienced members of the expedition decided to take off on their own, despite Muir's warning. When they failed to show up, he went after them, unconcerned about the threat of attack by warring Indian tribes.

"One I found deathlike, lying in the hot sand, scarcely conscious," he recalled. "The other I found in a kind of delirious stupor, voiceless, in the sagebrush. It was a fearfully exciting search, and I forgot my own exhaustion in it, though I never for a moment . . . doubted our ability to endure and escape. . . . Two days and nights in this fire without water!" For some time Muir and the two men he rescued were unable to swallow food and were kept sleepless by fever.

Unafraid of Indians, deserts, or cliff ascents, Muir felt terrified by the audiences who came to hear the accounts of his explorations. One friend observed, "He preferred a wilderness of wild beasts to a formal audience." Despite his stage fright, Muir captivated most of his audiences with his earnest, vivid, informative talks, and his modest, homespun manner.

Through Jeanne Carr he met Louie Wanda Strentzel, daughter of fruit farmers in Martinez, sixteen miles north of Oakland. A quiet, intelligent woman, Louie was an enthusiastic botanist, flower gardener, feminist, and amateur astronomer. Muir was definitely interested in her but wary, suspecting that a trap had been set to snare him from his bachelorhood. His suspicions were correct. Jeanne had secretly selected Louie as the ideal wife for the woman-shy mountaineer.

But at the age of forty Muir, the indefatigable bachelor, began to feel pangs of loneliness during his wanderings and expeditions. By the spring of 1879 he had made many visits to the Strentzel ranch, Louie Wanda being the chief reason. Now he finally summoned up courage enough to propose. Louie accepted, and their marriage was scheduled for the following spring, so that Muir could first take a long-dreamed-of trip to Alaska.

That summer he sailed on the first of five voyages of exploration and discovery in the mountains and glaciers of the Northwest Territory. He became the first white explorer to see Glacier Bay, which would later become a national monument. He also discovered a great ice river which was later named after him—Muir Glacier—and which he returned to on later trips. Muir himself was renamed by the native people, who called him "the Great Ice Chief."

From the skipper of a river steamer, Muir learned of fraudulent methods the lumber companies used to seize vast tracts of land in the Northwest.

On board he met a young resident missionary, S. Hall Young, who was in awe of the naturalist and eagerly joined him on a glacier climb. Climbing with Muir, Young slipped to a ledge overhanging the glacier. Hearing his cry, Muir worked his way below the ledge, seized Young by the belt and trouser seat, and lowered him step by step safely to the glacier.

· **TEN** ·

MUIR RETURNED EXHILARATED BY his adventure in January, 1880, and married Louie Wanda Strentzel that April. He settled down with her on her family's farm to raise fruit, lecture, and write magazine articles for sums that now reached $250 each, high pay for the time. "That I could earn money simply with written words," he marveled, "seemed very strange."

Muir spent most of the year hard at work on the farm. But between July and October, Louie agreed, he could wander on naturalist expeditions to his heart's content.

His trips to the Alaskan glaciers increased his knowledge of glaciation and provided more confirmation of his theories about the formation of the Sierras. The trips also swelled his spirit with emotion.

"The nearest glacier in particular," he wrote once, "was so distinct that it seemed to be glowing with light that came from within itself. . . . On this mountain-top, amid so much ice, in the heart of so clear and frosty a night, everything was more or less luminous, and I seemed to be poised in a vast hollow between two skies of almost equal brightness. This exhilarating scramble made me glad and strong and I rejoiced."

Though Muir had no interest in what he described as "$ geology," he was well versed on the subject. On his second trip to Alaska he pointed out a likely gold-bearing creek bed to two prospectors who did, indeed, strike gold. Muir had inadvertently started a gold rush that would lead to the founding of Juneau. It was on this Alaska trip that Muir's adventure with the dog Stickeen occurred.

Perhaps owing to his strenuous expeditions and exhausting labors on the farm, Muir fell ill with a bronchial cough and chronic indigestion. His narrow frame grew thinner, and Louie and his friends worried about his health. He seemed to recover, however, when his first child, Anna Wanda, was born in 1881.

"And never since the Glacial Period or Baby Period began on earth," he wrote a friend, "were happier people. How beautiful the world is and how beautiful is the time of the coming of our darling!"

Muir worked with conservationists in shaping two Congressional bills, one enlarging the Yosemite Valley reserve to include timber and water resources, the other setting aside a tract of California land as a public park. Both bills were quickly killed in the Senate by lumber and railroad lobbies intent on exploiting public lands for profit.

In the summer of 1884, John Muir took Louie on their first wilderness trip together in Yosemite. Louie was no mountaineer, however, and John had to prod her into ascending a peak. She was irked by his roughness, and he was annoyed by her ineptitude, so both decided it would be best if he climbed without her.

One day in 1885 John, who had not seen his father for eighteen years, had a sudden premonition that his father was dying. He hurried to Kansas City, where his ailing father was living with a married daughter. John summoned his brothers and sisters to his father's bedside.

Two weeks after the family gathered, Daniel Muir died. John wept, despite his hard feelings toward his father. His sister Joanna told him that their father had once admitted to her that he had made serious mistakes in handling his children, especially "my poor wandering son John." Skeptical scientist though he was, Muir couldn't help wondering about the inexplicable premonition that had brought him to his father's deathbed.

His second daughter, Helen, was born frail in January 1886. Muir stayed at home for eighteen months helping to care for her.

When his little girls were old enough, Muir enjoyed taking them around nearby hills. He instilled in them his love of the wilderness—"Nature's school ... the one true University." When he taught them the names of plants, flowers, and animals, Wanda (as she was called) wanted to know why it was important to remember them.

"Well," he replied, "how would you like it if people didn't call you by *your* name?"

When Muir blamed the dull farmwork for making him ill, Louie realized that her husband needed the mountains, not their farm. Muir's ten years of work on the farm had made his family well-to-do, so Louie was able to sell off and lease most of their land. Now Muir was freed for his wilderness, to make new discoveries and report them in his writing and lectures.

· ELEVEN ·

ALWAYS HIKING ON FOOT, MUIR carried only a change of underwear and socks, a few toilet articles, a blanket, a loaf of bread, tea, a cup, a small kettle, matches, a knife, and an ice ax. He kept warm at night by building a fire. In rain or snow he sought shelter in a cave or under a cliff. He hiked all over the Sierras, studying glaciers, plants, and flowers, while keeping journals for the books he planned.

"You can get along without eating for eight or ten days," Muir wrote, "and it would do you good as long as you had water and all you had to do was melt snow for that, if you kept your fire going."

In June of 1889, Muir served as a Valley guide for Robert Underwood Johnson, editor of *Century* magazine, which was to publish some of Muir's best articles. Muir expressed his disgust to Johnson at the fenced cow pastures, butcher shops, saloons, lumberyards, pigsties, and rundown hotels that now littered Yosemite. Hiring mules, they climbed out of the Valley into the high country, where they also saw meadows damaged by sheep, and signs of illegal lumbering.

Johnson helped resurrect an old dream of Muir's: to create a national preserve on the federal land around the Valley, modeled after Yellowstone. If Muir would write two articles for the *Century* proposing it, Johnson offered to add editorial support and lobby friends in Congress.

From then on Muir devoted most of his time to the cause of conservation. "Wherever the white man goes," he wrote in the *Century* in 1890, "the groves vanish. . . . Every kind of destruction is moving on with excessive speed."

Public response to his articles was tremendous. With Johnson's help, a bill was promptly introduced in Congress to create Yosemite National Park. At Muir's urging it included the beautiful Hetch Hetchy Valley. On October 1 the bill passed. Sheep ranching and lumbering were outlawed from 1,500 square miles of the Sierras. President William Harrison dispatched a U.S. Army cavalry patrol to enforce the restriction.

Elated by his success, Muir began fighting with his pen for more and more federal preservation of America's wilderness areas and its wildlife. Of course, he still made time for health- and soul-restoring wilderness expeditions. On one sled trip out to the Muir Glacier, Muir faced an attack by hungry wolves, beating them off with his walking staff. Later, Muir was soaked through when his sled broke through thin ice. Pulling himself out, he stripped, crept into his sleeping bag and "shivered the night away." Muir confided to his notebook, "It could have been worse."

Muir was less prepared for the savage attacks launched against him by cattlemen, sheep herders, lumbermen, and the Yosemite State and Turnpike Company, which ran tourist concessions in the Valley. After Muir's success in winning public support for the Yosemite bill, they saw the conservationist as their chief enemy. Newspaper editors and congressmen were flooded with letters accusing Muir of attempting to rob the state of its choicest treasures by turning them over to the federal government.

"Before he abandoned himself to profitable rhapsody and became a pseudo-naturalist," roared Oakland politician John P. Irish, "he cut and logged and sawed the trees of the Valley with as willing a hand as any lumberman in the Sierras!"

Muir's friends sprang to his defense, pointing out that he had sawn only trees already felled by storms. Muir himself called the accusation a lie, declaring, "I never cut down a single tree in the Yosemite, nor sawed a tree cut down by any other person there. Furthermore, I never held, or tried to hold any sort of claim in the Valley, or sold a foot of lumber there."

Depressed by the savagery of the attacks upon him, Muir doubted whether natural wonders could ever be permanently protected from powerful commercial interests. Robert Underwood Johnson also expected that those with a stake in exploiting wilderness areas would not cease attempts to rescind or curtail the Yosemite National Park bill, and would fight to prevent any similar bills. The editor of the *Century* asked Muir to form an association of nature-lovers who would fight back.

· TWELVE ·

JOHN MUIR WAS AN EFFECTIVE crusader and preacher for the gospel of the wilderness, but he was no organizer. He turned to Professor J. H. Senger of the University of California for help in uniting Californians who loved mountain travel. Early in 1892 Senger persuaded prominent attorney Warren Olney to organize a "Sierra Club." Muir promptly offered his support.

Begun on May 28, the club elected Muir president, a post he held until his death. Soliciting prospective members, he wrote them, "Do something for wildness and make the mountains glad."

A visitor staying at Muir's home recalled that he had never seen the mountaineer so happy "as when returning from organization meetings." Muir led the club's fight against big business efforts to reduce the area of Yosemite National Park by half. Calling for more national forest reserves, he urged members to "explore, enjoy and render accessible the mountain regions of the Pacific Coast." Meanwhile, Muir continued to write article after article appealing to the public to rescue more wilderness areas.

The impact of the Sierra Club was felt quickly. Before leaving office in 1893, President Harrison set aside another 13 million acres of watershed land as forest reserves, including the Sierra Forest Reserve. Lumbermen and sheep ranchers continued to trespass on these public lands, but most of the acreage was saved from destruction.

Muir's book *Mountains of California,* a revised collection of his published articles, came out in 1894. The fifty-six-year-old author was pleasantly astonished when the book achieved sales of ten thousand copies, excellent for those days.

The book helped persuade future president Theodore Roosevelt, then a U.S. Civil Service commissioner, of the need for conservation. He helped push the National Park Protective Act of 1894 through Congress.

The *Century* held a symposium to propose plans for training foresters and Army patrols to defend the reserves from poachers. Gifford Pinchot, a young conservationist, called for a U.S. Forest Service to protect and manage the forests, and when it was established he was credited as its founder. Pinchot claimed to be a great admirer of John Muir and sought his advice and guidance.

Muir advised him to plunge into the wilderness alone if he wished really to understand what it was that made preserving it a sacred obligation. Pinchot tried it "in a very small way," and confessed to Muir, "I am afraid that I shall never be able to do the amount of hard work that you have done, or get along on such slender rations."

When conservationists sought to have the Adirondack State Forest declared "forever wild," Pinchot fought the bill because it forbade lumbering. The two men also disagreed on other issues. An animal rights advocate ahead of his time, Muir defended the right to life of wild animals. Pinchot disagreed, echoing the popular opinion that there was no such thing as animal rights.

Leading arborist Charles Sprague Sargent warned Muir, "We have got to act promptly and secretly in these matters, or the politicians will overwhelm us." Pinchot would eventually prove to be one of those politicians.

Whenever Muir felt discouraged by setbacks to the cause of conservation, he could always lift his spirits by returning to the mountains. "The clearest way into the Universe," he wrote, "is through a forest wilderness. . . . Only by going alone in silence, without baggage, can one truly get into the heart of the wilderness. All other travel is mere dust and hotels and baggage and chatter. . . . One day's exposure to mountains is better than cartloads of books about them."

In 1896 Charles Sprague Sargent persuaded Muir to join him in a trip around the world. He tempted Muir with the promise of visits to the great forests of many nations. Muir's reputation as a mesmerizing speaker preceded him, and in Cairo, he was asked to deliver a talk on the giant sequoias of California. When he had finished, an Englishwoman rose to ask, "Would they make nice furniture?"

Horrified, Muir fixed her with a piercing gaze and demanded, "Madam, would you murder your own children?"

· THIRTEEN ·

WHEN HE RETURNED FROM HIS TRIP, Muir was asked to join a commission of the National Academy of Sciences making a survey of Western forests, along with Sargent and Pinchot.

Muir and Sargent demanded that the reserves should be kept inviolate, but Pinchot insisted upon their regulated use by commercial interests. The commission report recommended that the Grand Canyon and Mount Rainier be made new national parks, with thirteen new national forests. A compromise provision recommended that patrols be used to ban sheep grazing, but lumbering and mineral exploration were not prohibited.

President Grover Cleveland set aside lands for the national forests in February 1897. However, pressure by congressional lobbies of angry lumbermen, sheepmen, cattlemen, and mining interests forced cancellation of the presidential decree. The forest reserves were opened up to commercial claims.

Pinchot defended this setback for conservation by calling it "the greatest good for the greatest number." Muir replied in a *Harper's Weekly* article, "The greatest number is too often found to be number one. . . . Complaints are made in the name of poor settlers and miners, while the wealthy corporations are kept carefully hidden in the background."

After recommending that sheep and lumbering be allowed in the reserves, Pinchot was appointed head of the forestry division of the Agriculture Department. Sargent accused him of "selling out the forests" for a political appointment.

"What are we to do about forest matters?" Muir asked Sargent dolefully. "I mean simply to go on hammering and thumping as best I can at public opinion."

In May 1899 Muir was invited to join the Harriman Alaska Expedition for a two-month voyage. Scientists on the expedition praised the scientific use to which railroad magnate Harriman was putting his great wealth.

"I don't think Mr. Harriman is very rich," Muir interjected. "He has not as much money as I have. I have all I want, and Mr. Harriman has not." His indifference to money also appeared on another occasion, when he reflected upon his own early genius as an inventor. "I might have become a millionaire," he mused. "I chose instead to become a tramp."

In 1901 Muir published *Our National Parks,* another compilation of his magazine articles. It established him as the major voice of the American wilderness—"the Man of the Mountains." "I have done the best I could," he wrote, "to show forth the beauty, grandeur, and all-embracing usefulness of our wild mountain forest reservations and parks with a view to inciting the people to come and enjoy them, and get them into their hearts so that at length their preservation and right use might be made sure."

Honors were showered upon Muir. Harvard and the University of Wisconsin awarded him honorary degrees. One of the major Yosemite canyons was named Muir Gorge. Despite his renown, Muir remained a modest man, once describing himself as a mountaineer whose life was largely uneventful.

At age sixty-three he retained an astonishing vigor, with only minor changes in his appearance to reflect his new status. His hair and beard were still full, but now neatly trimmed. His clothes still hung on him like an unmade bed, but even on camping trips he now wore business suits.

He still felt bewildered by cities. When it was necessary to leave the wilderness to meet editors or attend functions, he worried about becoming corrupted by city luxuries like soft beds, heated rooms in winter, French bread, and fine coffee.

In 1901, to Muir's delight, Theodore Roosevelt became the first full-fledged conservationist in the White House. A friend wrote Muir, "The President is heartily with us in the matter of preserving the forests and keeping out the sheep. He wants to know the facts and is particularly anxious to learn them from men like yourself who are not connected with the Government service and at the same time are known and esteemed by the people."

Roosevelt declared, "The forest and water problems are

perhaps the most vital questions of the United States at the present time. . . . I recognize the right and duty of this generation to develop and use the natural resources of our land; but I do not recognize the right to waste them, or to rob by wasteful use, the generations that come after us." He created the Bureau of Forestry to manage the reserves, superseding the forestry division of the Agriculture Department.

Muir became upset with his Sierra Club because, while it agitated for conservation, it never took its members into the mountains. "Our Sierra Club seems half dead," he said wryly. He finally persuaded one hundred Club members to join him and his grown daughters in a month's camping trip through Yosemite.

"The Club outing is a great success," he wrote his wife from "Camp Muir." "God's ozone sparkles in every eye." The trip was so popular that the Sierra Club began to organize national park trips every summer. Membership doubled in just three years after the first trip.

In the spring of 1903, Roosevelt planned a trip through the West and wanted Muir to guide him through Yosemite. "I do not want anyone with me but you," the president wrote Muir, "and I want to drop politics absolutely for four days and just be out in the open with you."

· FOURTEEN ·

MUIR WROTE SARGENT, "AN influential man from Washington wants to make a trip into the Sierra with me, and I might be able to do some forest good in freely talking around the campfire."

When the presidential train was expected at night on May 3, Muir was advised to stay up to greet Roosevelt upon arrival. Muir shook his head. "Not for the President or any man will I lose my sleep."

Reporters mobbed him for details of the planned trip. Muir simply shrugged, "After we get to the Valley, the President and I will get lost."

On horseback, with a cook and two packers, he led Roosevelt into the Valley. He captivated the president with beautiful scenes of Yosemite's great peaks, valleys, and forests. At night they ate beefsteak and lay on Army blankets around a crackling campfire. Here Muir emphasized how important the Valley's forests and water resources were to all the people. "I stuffed him pretty well," he recalled later, "regarding the timber thieves, and the destructive work of the lumbermen, and other despoilers of the forests."

Once when the president began talking about shooting big game, Muir interrupted him brashly. "Mr. Roosevelt, when are you going to get beyond the boyishness of killing things?"

Startled, the president replied sheepishly, "Muir, I guess you are right." Subsequently he acknowledged to a reporter, "The older I grow the less I care to shoot anything except 'varmints.' . . . I am still something of a hunter, although a lover of wild nature first."

The president told a later chronicler of his camping trip with the California mountaineer, "Muir's deep solicitude over the destruction of our great forests and scenery made a deep impression on my mind. I came away with a greatly quickened conviction that vigorous action had to be taken speedily, before it should be too late."

Roosevelt agreed with famous naturalist John Burrough's observation that "John Muir talked even better than he wrote. His greatest influence was always upon those who were brought into personal contact with him."

Muir's memorable three nights of campfire talks with the president bore long-standing results. One day later Roosevelt

*President Theodore Roosevelt and John Muir
at Glacier Point, 1903.*
(Photograph courtesy of William E. Colby Memorial Library, Sierra Club)

extended the Sierra reserve northward all the way to Mount Shasta. Subsequently he set aside 150 million acres of timberland as national reserves, established fifty game preserves, doubled the number of national parks, and founded sixteen national monuments, the greatest saving of public lands accomplished by any president.

Muir threw himself into the fight to take the Yosemite Valley floor away from the mismanagement of corrupt state politicians. But bills to add it to the surrounding national park were blocked by the Southern Pacific stagecoach companies and hotels serving Valley tourists. Then Roosevelt threw his support behind the bills, while Muir's Sierra Club went to work on state and federal legislators. After an exhausting two-year battle, Muir and the conservationists finally won.

Worn out by the protracted struggle, Muir wrote *Century* editor Johnson, "Now that the fight is finished, and my education as a politician and lobbyist is finished, I am almost finished myself." But there was still no rest for him.

In 1905 the city of San Francisco demanded of the federal government that the Hetch Hetchy Valley be dammed to provide the city with free water power. Since this valley was within Yosemite National Park, the city needed federal permission.

"This Yosemite fight promises to be the worst ever," Muir wrote Johnson. He camped for a week in Hetch Hetchy, gathering material for articles and letters to fight against the destruction of the valley. He sighed, "This business won't even let me sleep." The battle against the dam continued for years.

Muir was upset when Roosevelt, for political reasons, appointed Gifford Pinchot head of the newly organized U.S. Forest Service. Pinchot promptly promised the lumber companies that their supply of timber would not be threatened. He also organized a Governors' Conference on natural resources to which hundreds of experts, but neither Muir nor most leading other conservationists, were invited.

In August 1905, Muir's wife Louie died, and his daughter Helen contracted pneumonia that left her lungs permanently affected. Living alone in his big house, Muir tried to blot out his grief by working on a book about his Alaskan explorations. Nothing restored his spirits as much as "going to the woods"—his beloved Yosemite.

Some time later he led a group, including John Burroughs, to the Grand Canyon. One night while they camped, Burroughs objected to staying up to talk about the canyon's natural wonders, saying he was sleepy and wanted only to go to bed.

"Sleepy, Johnnie!" Muir scoffed. "Why, lad, there'll be time to sleep . . . in the grave."

Bringing the party to the edge of the canyon, he exclaimed, "There! Empty your heads of all vanity, and look!"

One naturalist with the group marveled, "To think of having the Grand Canyon—and John Burroughs and John Muir thrown in!"

"I sometimes wish Muir *was* thrown in," Burroughs growled. Later he wrote Muir, "You are a dear anyway, Scotch obstinacy and all, and I love you, though at times I want to punch you or thrash the ground with you!"

Subsequently Burroughs wrote an article once more attacking Muir's theory that a prehistoric glacier had created Yosemite Valley. Muir replied caustically, "You saw so little of the Valley I think you should say little or nothing on its origin. . . . Compare this haphazard brazen ignorance with the careful loving lifelong bird studies that made you famous. You must be growing daft."

· FIFTEEN ·

WHEN WILLIAM HOWARD TAFT became president in 1909, he recognized that the exploitation of land and natural resources by commercial interests posed grave danger to the nation's supply of water, timber, minerals, and farmland. Like Roosevelt, he asked Muir to guide him on a trip through Yosemite.

Muir agreed eagerly, hoping to influence the president to support the continuing battle against allowing Hetch Hetchy to be ruined by a dam. Because Taft weighed 320 pounds, he was too heavy for horseback, so Muir took him to vantage points in the park on foot.

The president could not resist teasing the overly serious mountaineer. Once he observed with a straight face that the Valley would make a splendid farm. And pointing to a neck of the canyon, he said, "Now that would be a fine place for a dam!"

Horrified, Muir stuttered, "A dam! . . . The man who would dam that would be damning himself!"

Laughing, Taft assured Muir that he was only kidding, and that he opposed the Hetch Hetchy dam project. His support helped prevent the dam, for the time being.

At the age of seventy-three, Muir finished two more books, *The Yosemite* and *The Story of My Boyhood and Youth*. He rewarded himself with trips to South America and South Africa to study their forests. "The world's big," he told a friend, "and I want to have a good look at it before it gets dark."

He made two more trips through Yosemite in 1912. The next year was spent writing another book and leading the Sierra Club fight against the Hetch Hetchy dam. But this became a losing battle under the new White House occupant. Woodrow Wilson supported San Francisco's plan to dam the valley for water power.

John Muir reading the rocks, 1910.
(*From* Voices for the Earth: A Treasury of the Sierra Club Bulletin)

The dam builders won out in December 1913. The scenic masterpiece that was Hetch Hetchy Valley was drowned in dam water. Bitterly Muir called the project not only "a monumental mistake, but a monumental crime." Leading newspapers and magazines agreed, calling the dam a precedent for the commercial invasion of the national parks.

The exhausting battle to save Hetch Hetchy, only to end in defeat, helped destroy Muir's now fragile health. After developing pneumonia, he died on December 24, 1914.

Two years after his death, a law was passed placing all national parks under one director, as Muir had urged. This director was ordered to "conserve the scenery and the natural and historic objects and the wild life" in the parks. The director and his successors carried out the lifelong aims and ideals of the man who went down in American history as the "Father of Our National Parks."

John Muir had begun his struggle to preserve the natural beauty of America as a lone voice in the wilderness. But he ended as the guiding spirit of an organization of dedicated conservationists—the Sierra Club, which today numbers over 650,000 members.

It was Muir more than anyone else whose vision brought into being Yosemite National Park and presidential decrees setting aside other huge tracts of woodlands as national reserves. In recognition of his great contribution, his name has been immortalized in many of our states, including Mount Muir (California), Muir Point (Alaska), and Muir Glacier (Washington).

It was John Muir who challenged the conceit that humans owned the earth, all its creatures, plants, and forests, and could exploit them for profit. To Muir everything in nature was interconnected and sacred, to be loved, cherished, and preserved down through the generations, for as long as the earth should last.

Never before or since have we been blessed with so pure and dedicated a naturalist as Muir, who slid down glaciers for the sheer joy of it and climbed treetops in storms to ride the wind and view the spectacle of nature in all its awesome majesty.

Rachel Carson at the microscope, 1951.
(Brooks Studio photograph, used by permission of Rachel Carson History Project)

Rachel Carson

1 9 0 7 – 1 9 6 4

*"There Would Be No Peace for Me
If I Kept Silent"*

· ONE ·

IN JANUARY 1958 RACHEL CARSON received a thought-provoking letter from Olga Owens Huckins, a friend who had created a private bird sanctuary in Massachusetts. Huckins told Rachel that crop-duster planes had sprayed her neighborhood with DDT to kill mosquitoes. But the DDT had also killed a dozen songbirds and robins nesting in her garden and many in nearby woods, along with grasshoppers, bees, and other insects.

Huckins urged Rachel to use her influence as a nature writer to stop the lethal air spraying of DDT. Ten years earlier Rachel had tried to persuade *Reader's Digest* to publish an article about the dangers of pesticides and other long-lasting poison sprays used in agriculture. But the magazine had not been interested. Now Huckins's letter spurred Rachel to make a new attempt to save the environment from poisonous pesticides and herbicides causing wholesale destruction of wildlife and its habitat. At the same time she also felt impelled to sound an alarm about toxic wastes polluting the nation's land, air, and water.

"In a letter written in January 1958," Carson related in her book, *Silent Spring*, "Olga Owens Huckins told me of her own bitter experience of a small world made lifeless, and so brought my attention sharply back to a problem with which I had long been concerned. I then realized I must write this book."

The title *Silent Spring* was chosen by her editor, Paul Brooks, from Carson's opening fable of a town where no bird-songs were heard: "It was a spring without voices. On the mornings that had once throbbed with the dawn chorus of robins, catbirds, doves, jays, wrens and scores of other bird voices there was now no sound: only silence lay over the fields and woods and marsh."

The research reported in Carson's book was to engage her in major battles with powerful enemies of conservation. United States chemical companies had assured the government that their pesticides were harmless to humans, animals, and the creatures living in lakes, rivers, and oceans. Rachel Carson undertook exhaustive research to prove them wrong. Her battle established her firmly as the founder of the modern ecology movement, compelling the government to take steps to protect the environment.

· T W O ·

RACHEL CARSON WAS BORN ON May 27, 1907, in Springdale, Pennsylvania, a small town on the Allegheny River, twelve miles upstream from the smoke-belching steel mills of Pittsburgh. She grew up on her father's sixty-five-acre farm, surrounded by woods and the pretty countryside that first shaped her love of nature.

"I was rather a solitary child," she recalled, "and spent a great deal of time in woods and beside streams, learning the birds and the insects and the flowers." Because her brother Robert was eight years older, and her sister Marian ten years older, they were not playmates for Rachel. She lived too far from neighbors to have other children as friends. In the early 1900s very few Americans had cars, and country roads were often too muddy for horse-drawn buggies.

Rachel was often accompanied in her explorations of fields and forests by her mother, Maria. A former schoolteacher, Maria would take her daughter into the woods at dawn to listen to the first birdsongs. Together they took long nature walks, observing the world of ants, butterflies, bees, garter snakes, and spiders and their fascinating webs. Maria, who would release insects outdoors rather than kill them in her house, instilled in her daughter a reverence and compassion for all forms of wildlife.

Once Rachel and her mother came upon a destroyed bird's nest with apparently abandoned baby robins. At Rachel's urging, her mother took the fledglings home, feeding them by hand every few hours. The babies thrived and soon made the Carsons' screened porch their aviary. Rachel kept everyone in the family out of the porch until the birds could fly well enough to return to the forest.

Rachel developed an insatiable curiosity on their nature walks and was constantly plying her mother with questions. If Maria didn't know the answers, she would encourage her inquisitive daughter to consult science books. Rachel loved to read, not just about science, but also animal stories and stories of the sea.

"As a very small child," Rachel declared years later, "I was fascinated by the ocean, though I had never seen it. I dreamed of it and longed to see it." Rachel liked to listen to the soft roar she heard when she put her mother's beautiful pink conch shell to her ear.

"Some people think what you hear is the sound of ocean waves," her mother told her with a smile. "It's not, but it does sound a lot like it." Still, even this hint of what the sea might sound like inspired Rachel's imagination.

A quiet, shy, small child who relished thoughtful walks through the woods alone, Rachel was not sure she would enjoy the change when it was time for her to attend school. In September 1913 her mother took her to the Springdale Grammar School. Rachel's attendance was sporadic because her mother feared Rachel might become ill on her long walk to school, and so kept her home frequently, especially during the winter months when a flu epidemic was raging.

Rachel's grades did not suffer, because her mother tutored her at home so well that teachers who called on Rachel in class rarely caught her without the correct answer. Her teachers were impressed by the poems Rachel began writing when she was only eight, and they encouraged her to keep writing.

Rachel's love of the magic of books never waned. It wasn't long before she had gone through every book in the Carson home, even those she couldn't fully understand. She begged to be taken to the library in the family horse and buggy whenever her father rode into town.

"I read a good deal," she said later, "and I suppose I must have realized someone wrote the books, and thought it would be fun to make up stories, too."

When America entered World War I in 1917, Rachel's brother Robert joined the U.S. Army Air Service in Texas. Rachel read his letters home eagerly, fascinated by the details of a world so removed from her sheltered life. She was thrilled by one letter in particular, Robert's report of a Canadian flier's exceptional bravery during an air duel with German aviators.

St. Nicholas Magazine, then the most prestigious children's periodical, had been urging its young readers to write brief articles for its St. Nicholas League contest about the bravery of fighter pilots. Inspired by Robert's story, Rachel set out to relate it, rewriting many times before she was satisfied. She showed it to her mother, who judged it good enough to submit. Rachel mailed the story off, then searched for it with beating heart in each new issue of *St. Nicholas.*

Each month that she was disappointed made Rachel feel that her hopes of becoming a writer were unrealistic. Then when she opened the September 1918 issue, she found her story. "A Battle in the Clouds," by Rachel L. Carson (Age 10), was awarded the magazine's silver badge for excellence. She also received her first pay as a professional author—ten dollars.

To prove to herself that her first success was no fluke, Rachel submitted a second war article, "A Message to the Front." Appearing in the February 1919 issue, it was awarded the magazine's gold badge. A third article, "A Famous Sea Fight," about Admiral Dewey's victory in the Spanish-American War, appeared six months later. By this time an elated Rachel was convinced of her ability to pursue a writing career.

She worked hard at school to earn the grades that would eventually open college doors to her. Rachel earned high marks at Springdale High and Parnassus High School, where she was often asked by teachers to read her compositions aloud. At this time, only a small minority of women entered college. But her teachers, impressed with Rachel's earnestness and writing ability, encouraged her lofty aspiration.

The college Rachel chose was Pennsylvania College for Women (later Chatham College). But money was an obstacle. Her splendid academic record was rewarded with only a partial scholarship. Rachel had to go into debt to go to college.

As a freshman she quickly became one of the top ten students in her class. While her classmates, many from wealthy families, engaged in a social whirl, Rachel closeted herself in the library or in her room, writing. Other students regarded the quiet, soft-spoken girl as just "not social." Part of the reason Rachel held apart from social activities was that she could not afford them. She began to reach out for friends in her sophomore year by joining the college field hockey team. Yet she was embarrassed not to be able to join them after practice at a soda parlor. The fifteen-cent price of a soda was more than her budget allowed.

At first, Rachel's major was English, since she was determined to become a writer. She worked on the college newspaper and yearbook, and one of her stories was published in the college literary magazine. But at eighteen, when she had to write an essay called "Who I Am," she realized that writing was becoming less important to her than her preoccupation with an outdoor life.

Describing herself in the essay as "intensely fond of anything pertaining to outdoors and athletics," Rachel wrote, "I am seldom happier than when I am before a glowing campfire with the open sky above my head. I love all the beautiful things of nature, and the wild creatures are my friends."

Rachel's career plans were also affected by Professor Mary Skinker's biology class. Because biology had been very dull in high school, Rachel had dreaded it in college as a boring waste of time. She took it only because she needed the course to graduate.

She was surprised when Skinker proved an inspiring teacher who made biology seem the most fascinating subject in the world. Rachel's eyes were opened to the wonderful chain of life that linked the lowliest, single-celled creatures, invisible except under a microscope, to the largest creatures of the forest, and to humankind itself.

Skinker expanded Rachel's thinking as nothing had before. Rachel found herself devoting more of her time and energy to biology than to writing. The break from writing also seemed to end her isolation. In addition to playing hockey, she joined the baseball and basketball teams and joined in her fellow students' sledding parties on snowy nights. Her classmates found the formerly bookish and solitary Rachel as fond of fun as they were.

She continued to excel in biology as well as English and couldn't decide which to pursue as a major. Then one stormy night, reading Tennyson's poem "Locksley Hall" Rachel reached the line: "For the mighty wind arises, roaring seaward, and I go."

She dropped the book and stared at the torrents of rain streaking her window. Suddenly her old fascination with the sea, which she still had not seen, revived. She fell to musing about the wonderful world of the oceans, of the millions of life forms living beneath the waves.

That night Rachel made a decision that changed her whole life. She decided that biology, not writing, should become her new major and her future career.

"I can still remember, as that line spoke to something within me," she recalled in 1955, "seeming to tell me that my own path led to the sea . . . and that my own destiny was somehow linked with the sea."

· **THREE** ·

THE PRESIDENT OF THE COLLEGE was shocked by Rachel's decision to change her major. It was a sin to waste her writing talent, she reproached Rachel. Didn't Rachel realize that few women ever achieved anything in the "man's world" of biology and science? Her English teacher, Grace Croff, and her classmates also thought Rachel had made a ridiculous decision.

"I've gotten bawled out and called all sorts of blankety-blank names," she sighed. "Nobody can seem to understand why I'd give up English for biology."

But Rachel had made up her mind. She loved taking field trips with Skinker to forests, pools, and streams, collecting, dissecting, and studying specimens under the microscope. Also fascinated by the fossils she found, she speculated on how the landscape and life around her had changed over millions of years.

Looking back on these trips years later, she wrote, "On a

mountain top in Pennsylvania I have sat on rocks of whitened limestone, fashioned of the shells of billions upon billions of minute sea creatures. Once they had lived and died in an arm of the ocean that overlay this place, and their limy remains had settled to the bottom. There, after eons of time, they had become compacted into rock and the sea had receded; after yet more eons the rock had been uplifted by bucklings of the earth's crust and now it formed the backbone of a long mountain range."

To try to meet her mounting college debt, Rachel earned seventy-five dollars during the summer before her senior year by tutoring high school students. Her mother, who had already sold the family china and some home furnishings to pay for Rachel's tuition, scraped up another hundred dollars to make sure Rachel was allowed to continue. During her last year Rachel took no less than six science courses, achieving high marks in all. Elected president of a new college science club, she still found time for her friends and the hockey team.

In June 1929, just before the Depression set in, Rachel graduated *magna cum laude.* Mary Skinker recommended her for a summer scholarship at the Woods Hole Marine Biological Laboratory on Cape Cod. She also won a one-year scholarship for graduate study in zoology at Johns Hopkins University.

Rachel was thrilled at her good fortune. At Woods Hole she would be working with gifted scientists at one of the great oceanography facilities, right at the edge of the sea. The sea, at last!

Returning home, Carson burned with impatience waiting for her summer at Woods Hole to begin. She was disturbed by the changes she noticed in the countryside around Springdale. The Allegheny River was being lined with industrial plants whose huge smokestacks poured toxic wastes into the air.

There were more storage tanks for chemicals, oil, and natural gas than she remembered. The river looked dirty, polluted by industrial wastes and barge discharges.

Depressed by what had happened to her neighborhood, Carson felt relieved when it was time for her to leave. She traveled to Baltimore to register at Johns Hopkins, then went to Virginia to visit with vacationing Mary Skinker.

Traveling on to New York, she took a boat to New Bedford, Massachusetts, relishing her first view of the ocean. She could not get enough of inhaling the salt air, of watching the enormous watery horizon.

At New Bedford she transferred to a small boat which took her sixteen miles across Buzzards Bay to Woods Hole. As the boat pulled into the harbor, Carson stared in fascination at the buildings of the U.S. Bureau of Fisheries and the Marine Biological Laboratory. Here her new life as a scientist would begin.

Her six weeks studying at Woods Hole were happy ones. Scientists from the Bureau of Fisheries took her along with them on their marine expeditions. Carson found the ocean breathtaking, and was often moved to tears by its beauty. The soft silver sea fog that covered Woods Hole in the mornings before burning off by noon made her feel that she was living in some enchanted fairyland.

When she expressed her yearning to work at the Bureau of Fisheries, one scientist shook his head.

"There are no women scientists in the Bureau," he said.

"Perhaps some day there will be," she replied hopefully.

"You might talk to Elmer Higgins in Washington," he suggested. "He's head of the Division of Scientific Inquiry."

After her summer at Woods Hole, before going to Johns Hopkins, Carson stopped in Washington to see Higgins. He again told her that the only scientists at the Bureau were male.

About the only jobs open to women biologists, he advised her, were as high school and college teachers. *All* of the sciences, Higgins explained, were largely male-dominated.

"Not for long," Carson vowed silently. She was determined to find her niche in marine biology despite all odds.

· FOUR ·

AT JOHNS HOPKINS CARSON took chemistry and biology classes from breakfast to dinner, spending long hours in research and laboratory work.

The year was 1930, and the Depression had begun, bringing some of the hardest times Americans had ever known. At its height, fifteen million were jobless, and millions were able to survive only by waiting on long breadlines.

Carson found a house she could rent cheaply close to Baltimore and urged her parents to move from Springdale to live with her. Her sister Marian was married by now, and her brother Robert had a job in Pittsburgh. So her parents joined her, and remained with her for the rest of their lives. Because the family finances were perilous, Rachel found it necessary to take a job as a teaching assistant in biology at the Johns Hopkins summer school.

"I've just put in a tough day at the lab," she wrote to a friend. "Getting the lab ready for 45 students is no fun. I have to do everything myself. A lot of glassware needs washing, and I have to see to it that each table is supplied with a long list of apparatus." But she performed the job so diligently that she was rehired every summer through 1936.

When her second year began in the fall, she also took two jobs as a lab assistant. She still found time for a scientific project studying fish eggs that required long hours over a microscope and lengthy research in the library. Her 108-page report won her a master's degree in marine zoology.

On July 6, 1935, Carson's burdens increased when her father died of a heart attack. His odd jobs had helped the family stay afloat until now. She was faced with having to support her mother as well as herself. Moreover, her sister Marian was now divorced, and she and her two daughters moved in with Rachel. Her divorced brother Robert also moved in, taking odd jobs to help pay the rent.

Desperate for a job in a field that employed few women, Rachel decided to apply to Elmer Higgins at the U.S. Bureau of Fisheries. She was gratified that he remembered her. But he told her that he had no job for a biologist.

Suddenly he asked, "Can you write?"

"I majored in English before I switched to biology," she replied, "and got all straight A's in my English courses."

Higgins told her that the Bureau had undertaken fifty-two seven-minute radio broadcasts about marine life under the series title "Romance Under the Waters." The professional radio writer he had hired part-time had proved to be scientifically inept. And no staff scientist could write in a style interesting and comprehensible to nonscientists. Would Carson care to prove she could do the job by writing three test assignments?

The job was part-time and the pay only $19.25 a week, but in jobless 1935 that was survival money. Carson eagerly set to work on the three scripts.

When Higgins read her work, he looked at Carson with new respect. "You've got the job," he said. "You can work at home if you prefer, or in our department library."

"That little job," Carson recalled, "was, in its way, a turning point."

Determined to win a full-time job at the Bureau as a biologist, Carson took a civil service exam for the post of junior aquatic biologist, paying two thousand dollars a year. The only woman applicant, she scored higher than any of the men competing for the job. To her delight she was hired on August 17, 1936, one of the first two women ever to hold a professional civil service position at the Fish and Wildlife Service.

Higgins immediately asked to have her assigned to his office. To her disappointment, Carson found that her new job would still be not as a biologist but as a writer. She was required to turn out booklets for the bureau, and research and answer scientific questions people submitted to the bureau.

Higgins gave her the job of editing what they had come to call the "fish tale" broadcasts she had written into a pamphlet, with an introduction tying them together. When she showed him her introduction, called "Undersea," Higgins shook his head.

The trouble with it, he explained, was that it was so beautiful, colorful, and poetic in its descriptions of the sea that it made the fish tales themselves seem dull by comparison. Asking her to write a "simpler" introduction, he nevertheless suggested that she send what she had written to the *Atlantic Monthly.* Carson was astonished that he thought her essay good enough for one of the leading literary magazines in America. Unable to believe it, she simply put the essay away in a drawer.

Her new job and steady income let Carson and her mother move to a new two-story house in Silver Spring, Maryland, closer to Washington. When her sister Marian died of pneumonia, Rachel took care of her two small orphaned nieces, Marjie and Ginny. Her mother looked after them while Carson was at work. Carson often took her nieces to the Maryland woods and marshes to discover and enjoy the wildlife.

The added financial burden of raising her two nieces led Carson to try a long shot. Retrieving the discarded fish tales introduction from her desk drawer, she made some changes and asked her mother to retype it. Off it went to the *Atlantic Monthly*, as Higgins had suggested.

To her amazement, within two months she received a check for seventy-five dollars from the magazine with a letter advising her that "Undersea" would be published in the September 1937 issue.

A serious author at last!

· **FIVE** ·

CARSON RESISTED TELLING HIGGINS about the article until she had a copy of the issue. Then without a word she opened it to her article and placed it on his desk in front of him.

As she waited in excitement for his reaction, he read the article silently. He paused over a paragraph:

> To sense this world of waters known to the creatures of the sea we must shed our human perceptions of length and breadth and time and place, and enter vicariously into a universe of all-pervading water. For to the sea's children nothing is so important as the fluidity of their world. It is water that they breathe; water that brings them food; water through which they see, by filtered sunshine from which first the red rays, then the greens, and finally the purples have been strained; water through which they sense vibrations equivalent of sound.

Carson was chagrined when her boss once more shook his head as he handed her back the magazine.

"What's wrong with it *now?*" she stammered, vexed.

"What's wrong with it is that it ought to be a *book*," he replied, "not just a magazine article."

"A *book?* When could I write a book?"

"All you'd have to do is expand each paragraph into a chapter, and you'll have a book. Your article is actually an outline for the whole story of marine ecology."

The thought of trying to write a whole book intimidated Carson, so she again dismissed Higgins's advice. She had second thoughts, however, when the *Atlantic* article brought her two important letters. The first was from Hendrik Willem van Loon, celebrated author of the famous *History of Mankind*. He wrote that she had an unusual talent for writing about nature and should certainly expand "Undersea" into a book. He urged this project on his editor-in-chief at Simon & Schuster, Quincy Howe, who wrote to Carson proposing it.

Excited, Carson corresponded with both men. She arranged with Higgins for time off to accept van Loon's invitation to his Connecticut home to meet with him and Howe. Howe asked her to send him a detailed synopsis of what such a book would cover, along with a sample chapter.

Carson lost no time in plunging into the project on weekends and evenings. She undertook painstaking research to make absolutely certain of all her facts. Working diligently on the sample chapter, she sensed an exciting opportunity that might change the whole course of her life.

Despite the pressures of her writing and her job, Carson still made time to steal away for a few hours of soul-sustaining hiking and bird-watching, sometimes with her mother and nieces. For Carson, repeated exposure to nature was essential to her sense of serenity. It was as though she could not feel complete unless she bonded with wildlife.

Carson was disappointed when she submitted the outline

and chapter for her proposed book, *Under the Sea Wind,* and Howe asked to see a few more chapters. By early 1940, driving herself relentlessly, an exhausted Carson managed to finish four more chapters and dispatch them.

Shortly after, she received a contract with a $250 advance.

Thrilled, Carson worked late into the night, often falling asleep over her manuscript. Her book described how fish, birds, and sea mammals lived together in, over, and around their common home, the vast ocean. And Carson told the story from *their* viewpoint, not a human observer's, so that readers could enjoy the vicarious experience of living as one of them.

When the finished manuscript was in Quincy Howe's hands, it bore the simple heartfelt dedication "To my mother." Rachel never forgot that it had been Maria Carson who had first taught her to love the creatures of the forest, who had encouraged her ambitions as a writer and then as a scientist, who had typed all her final drafts, and who had looked after Marjie and Ginny while she worked.

When Carson received her copies of the finished book, she walked into her boss's office and handed him one. It was inscribed, "To Mr. Higgins, who started it all."

Despite good reviews, *Under the Sea Wind* sold poorly. It was December 1941 and America had just entered World War II. Everyone could talk and think of little else but the war, and had turned to reading newspapers instead of books. Carson was bitterly disappointed, for she had counted on royalties to repay her for three years of intensive research, hard work, and constant rewriting. But she received less than one thousand dollars for its sale of 1,348 copies.

"Don't ever write a book," she told a friend mournfully. "It doesn't pay as well as a single well-placed magazine article."

She directed all her energy back to her job at the Bureau

of Fisheries, now renamed the Fish and Wildlife Service. Her dedication and the quality of her work brought her three promotions in her first three years with the bureau.

The bureau's work rose to new national importance during the war. American warships and submarines needed accurate information about ocean depths, currents, tides, and wave action—a scientific study of the sea.

With the war effort siphoning off many men from the bureau, Carson became indispensable. In 1942 she was promoted to assistant to the chief of the Office of Information of the Fish and Wildlife Service, and transferred to a Chicago office for two years. Here she worked on a series of pamphlets on fish and diet. But again, Carson's writing talents were more in demand than her research abilities.

· SIX ·

AFTER THE WAR CARSON WAS transferred back to Washington and promoted to associate aquatic biologist. Her research took her to the shores of many states, and to wildlife refuges where she could study bird migrations.

Her companion on many of these field trips was her friend and co-worker Shirley Briggs. Describing their "high adventures," Briggs said, "We who were included in her own expeditions learned a great deal about many aspects of our world, but most of all a way of seeing, alert for every impression, with keen delight in all manner of small creatures." On trips along the shore, Carson also demonstrated her gift for mentally transforming herself into the sea creatures she studied, so that she could experience what they were experiencing.

On her travels for the Fish and Wildlife Service, Carson became increasingly aware of a growing threat to the natural resources she treasured. War production had caused increases

*Rachel Carson watching migrating hawks from
Hawk Mountain, Pennsylvania, 1945.*
(Photo by Shirley A. Briggs, used by permission of Rachel Carson History Project)

in pollution and the misuse and neglect of seacoasts, rivers, and forests. Overhunting had decimated deer herds. Overfishing had decreased fish in lakes and rivers. Farmlands and marshlands had been sacrificed to suburban developments and shopping malls, destroying the habitat of birds and animals. And pesticides and herbicides were causing wholesale destruction of wildlife.

Carson saw an urgent need to make Americans aware of the need to care about and preserve their natural environment, before other American wildlife became as scarce as the buffalo. She felt driven to write something dramatic that would wake up America to the growing crisis.

She tried to sell articles to magazines warning of the dangers of the indiscriminate use of pesticides and herbicides. But magazine publishers wouldn't accept her exposés, fearing that powerful chemical companies would be offended and drop their advertisements.

Finally Carson convinced the Fish and Wildlife Service to agree to publish a series of twelve booklets called *Conservation in Action.* Carson was to edit the series and write four or five of the booklets explaining the need for wildlife conservation. In her introduction to the series, she wrote an eloquent plea for humankind to live in harmony with nature and its creatures.

"Wild creatures, like men, must have a place to live," she declared. "As civilization creates cities, builds highways, and drains marshes it takes away, little by little, the land that is suitable for wildlife. And as their spaces for living dwindle, the wildlife populations themselves decline."

With her fortieth birthday approaching in 1947, she began feeling trapped by her job and frustrated in her literary career. "I write nothing," she fretted to Shirley Briggs, "and am fast coming to feel that I have lost what it takes to produce a companion to that first and solitary book. No, my life isn't at all well ordered and I don't know where I'm going."

Yet by 1948 she had been promoted to editor-in-chief of all Fish and Wildlife Service publications, with six assistants. It amused her to reflect that where once she had been told it was useless for a woman to aspire to government employment as a scientist, now one of her assistants was a man. He was Bob Hines, a wildlife artist who at first had been reluctant to serve under a woman supervisor. But when he met Carson he was greatly impressed.

"She was a very able executive," he said later. "She knew how to get things done the quickest, simplest, most direct way. She had the sweetest, quietest 'no' any of us had ever heard. But it was like Gibraltar. You didn't move it."

Carson and Hines became close associates and friends. He often accompanied her on field trips to sketch the creatures she wrote about. Some in the office thought their closeness might develop into a romantic relationship, but it never did. Although Carson once confided to a friend that she would like to get married, she did nothing to encourage any man's romantic interest in her.

"When she said she just never had time to get married," Shirley Briggs observed, "that's probably exactly right." And any total commitment outside of marriage was foreign to Carson's sense of morality.

· **SEVEN** ·

CARSON BEGAN WRITING A NEW BOOK, *The Sea Around Us,* in the summer of 1948. The book was intended "for anyone who has looked out upon the ocean with wonder from the deck of a liner or a troop transport, or has stood on the shore alone with the waves and his thoughts, or has felt from afar the fascination of the sea." She strove to make the book "easily understood and imaginatively appealing to the reader untrained in science." She hoped that such a book on oceanography would win readers over to the cause of conservation, especially the need to fight pollution of the seas and the rivers that fed into them.

Carson put into the book all the research she had done traveling along the Atlantic seaboard and off the coast of California. She often worked on it at home through the predawn hours, after spending a full day at the Fish and Wildlife Service.

Within six months she had enough of the book completed to show to a literary agent, Mrs. Marie Rodell, in New York. Rodell won a contract for her with Oxford University Press, but there was one hitch: Oxford demanded the whole manuscript within ten months. And it had taken Carson three years to write *Under the Sea Wind*. Despite being able to work on it only at nights and on weekends, she determined to do her best to meet the deadline.

In addition to consulting over a thousand printed reference sources, Carson corresponded extensively with experts in oceanography. The work was so exhausting that more than once she reproached herself for undertaking so overwhelming a task. Her home life did not make the task easier. Carson had to care for her mother, now in her late seventies, and she herself suffered frequent bouts of illness.

"She kept on going as best she could," Shirley Briggs said.

"I can't possibly finish it by the deadline," Rachel finally told her agent. Rodell suggested that she get a writing grant, which would let her take a leave of absence from her job to write the book full-time. On the recommendations of famous oceanographer Dr. William Beebe and naturalist Edwin Way

Tearle, both admirers of Carson's writing, she received a $2,250 fellowship grant from the Sexton Memorial Fund.

Dr. Beebe, a deep-sea diver with whom Carson had enjoyed a correspondence since the publication of her first article, "Undersea," advised her that to write a perceptive book about underwater life, she really needed to go underwater and experience it herself. She took up her friend's challenge. But these were the days before scuba gear, when diving required a helmet, foot weights, and air pumped down to the diver through a hose—and Carson wasn't even a good swimmer!

She took the first of several underwater dives with the Fish and Wildlife Service, from which she was now on leave, off the Florida coast in July 1949. She later wrote of the dives, "There I learned what the surface of the water looks like from underneath and how exquisitely delicate and varied are the colors displayed by the animals of the reef, and I got the feeling of the green vistas of a strange, non-human world." She told Shirley Briggs that her first dive had been one of the greatest moments of her life, "after which everything seems a little different."

Accompanied by Marie Rodell, she boarded the service's research vessel, *Albatross III,* for an expedition to collect sea samples, becoming the first woman to join the ship's fifty-man team. Out of sight of land for ten days, Carson developed a new sense of the vast expanse and ceaseless movements of the sea.

The food was terrible, and it was hard to keep from getting seasick. The endless clanking of the ship's machinery and chains day and night made the expedition anything but a pleasure cruise. But Carson gained invaluable information and insights which added to the value of her book.

The smallness of her grant soon compelled her to return to her job. New drains on her time and energy occurred when one

Rachel Carson on a 1949 shallow-diving trip, on the University of Miami research boat Nauplius, *with a copper diving helmet.*
(Photo by Shirley A. Briggs, used by permission of Rachel Carson History Project)

of her nieces fell ill, and when she and the family had to move to a new house in Silver Spring. Through it all, by sacrificing her morning birdwatching walks, Carson persisted at her typewriter. She groaned to Marie Rodell, "I feel now that I'd die if this went on much longer." But at last a final draft of the book, typed by her mother, reached the publisher in July 1950, several months late.

The Sea Around Us described in fascinating detail the ecology of the ocean. Ecology, meaning a study of plant life and animals with reference to their environment, was not a familiar term in the 1950s. For many of her readers, Carson's book presented a completely new way of looking at the interconnections of the natural world. It also revealed the seas to be a far more diverse and complex habitat than they could have imagined. Readers learned about the miles-deep water canyons where strange sea creatures lived under great pressure, and about the continental shelves that provided humankind with great fisheries, medicinal seaweeds, and underwater oilfields.

When Carson received advance copies of her book, she presented one to her illustrator friend Bob Hines, who had constantly carried heavy armloads of research books for her back and forth from the library. It was inscribed, "To Bob Hines, who bore many of the burdens connected with the writing of this book."

Dreading that *The Sea Around Us* would quickly sink into oblivion like her first book, Carson was amazed and gratified when, just one month after publication in July 1951, it was already a best-seller. And it stayed on the best-seller list for almost two years.

Her book made understandable the behavior of ocean currents in all parts of the world, and their effects on fish and weather. She explained how tides behaved, and how they affected the sea, sea creatures, and shipping. She showed how studies of wave action had been important in planning World War II invasions of enemy lands, and how they helped save ships from sea storms as well as save lives on shore from hurricanes.

To Carson the sea was "that great mother of life," the watery cradle where all life had begun, and which provided life for trillions of creatures. She reminded readers that humanity had been in existence for a very small part of the earth's history, and that "this world is a water world, a planet dominated by its covering mantle of ocean, in which the continents are but transient intrusions of land above the surface of the all-encircling sea."

· EIGHT ·

SCIENCE ORGANIZATIONS AND BOOK reviewers had nothing but praise for the book. Magazines paid high fees for the rights to reprint parts of it. Honorary degrees were showered on Carson by Oberlin College, the Drexel Institute for Technology, and Smith College. She suddenly found herself famous and in great demand as a speaker at luncheons, universities, and book signings.

Those who heard her speak were greatly taken by her modest, quiet, but confident manner. Still shy, however, she found it difficult to speak with all the people who crowded around, eager to engage her in conversation. They were intrigued by the brilliant scientist who had been able to break through the dull language of aquatic biology to make the wonders of ocean science clear and exciting to nonscientists.

To escape the exhaustion which an operation and sudden fame had thrust upon her, and to regain some privacy, Carson retreated to Beaufort, North Carolina, for a week of scientific beachcombing. "The truth is," she sighed to a friend, "I'm much more at home barefoot in the sand or on shipboard in sneakers than . . . in high heels."

The Guggenheim Foundation awarded her a working fellowship and four-thousand-dollar grant, allowing her to take another leave of absence from her job to write a third book.

In January 1952, Carson received the first medal ever awarded to a woman by the Philadelphia Geographical Society. She also won a National Book Award gold medallion for the best nonfiction book of the year, and was asked to speak at the ceremony.

"Many people have commented with surprise," she said, "on the fact that a work of science should have such a large popular sale. . . . We live in a scientific age. . . . Science is part of the reality of living; it is the what, the how, and the why of everything in our experience. . . . If there is poetry in my book about the sea, it is . . . because no one could write truthfully about the sea and leave out the poetry."

There seemed no end to the impact of *The Sea Around Us*. Oxford University Press climbed on the Carson bandwagon by reissuing her first book, *Under the Sea Wind*, which quickly climbed onto the best-seller list.

Book royalties, awards, magazine payments, and lecture fees were pouring in, making Carson realize that she now could realize her dream of making a living solely by writing books.

In June 1952 she officially resigned from the Fish and Wildlife Service.

· **NINE** ·

CARSON PAID OFF ALL HER DEBTS, and also returned the Guggenheim grant. She had a cottage built for herself and her mother at the shore in West Southport, Maine. Her two nieces, grown by this time, now lived on their own.

From the desk in her new workroom, Carson could view the ocean, sky, and woods. Steps led down to the beach, where she and her mother often fed the sea gulls by hand.

She did not retreat to an ivory tower, however, remaining active as a conservationist. In Washington she had been director of the local Audubon Society board and had written conservation speeches for congressmen. In Maine she helped organize a chapter of the Nature Conservancy.

When she began writing her new book, *The Edge of the Sea,* Carson's goal was "to take the seashore out of the category of scenery and make it come alive." What fascinated Carson was that the seashore below high tide belonged "now to the land, now to the sea . . . a place where the dramatic process of evolution can actually be observed." This tideland demanded "every bit of adaptability living things can muster."

Paul Brooks, Carson's editor at Houghton Mifflin, joined her on some of her research excursions. He recalled one evening after they'd studied sea creatures under her microscope.

"Then," he wrote, "pail and flashlight in hand, she stepped carefully over the kelp-covered rocks to return the living creatures to their home. This, I think, is what [noted humanitarian] Albert Schweitzer . . . meant by reverence for life. In one form or another it lies behind everything that Rachel Carson wrote." Significantly, Carson dedicated a later book, *Silent Spring,* to "Albert Schweitzer, who said, 'Man has lost the capacity to foresee and forestall. He will end by destroying the earth.'"

Oblivious of mosquitoes, Carson would often stand bent over for hours in Maine's freezing tidepools in her bare feet. Sometimes she became so numb that Bob Hines, who joined Carson to make sketches for the book, would have to carry her back to her car in his arms, like the load of library books he had trundled for her during research for *The Sea Around Us.*

She would trick ghost shrimp into appearing by dropping grains of sand down their burrows. Exploring Florida sea worms, she found a species that until then had been known only in the Pacific and Indian oceans, and tried to imagine how they could have migrated across the land barrier of two continents.

It did not faze her to be in waters with barricuda, stingrays, and Portuguese men-of-war that sometimes navigated around her. "In sudden movements, swirling waters, and half-seen shadows that dart across my path as I wade shoreward," she wrote, "I sense the ancient drama of the strong against the weak."

Whenever she walked along the beach at low tide, Carson was always conscious that she was "treading on the thin rooftops of an underground city. . . . The inhabitants remain hidden, dwelling silently in their dark, incomprehensible world." It was this special awareness of vast worlds other than human that made Carson unique among biologists. Fascinated, she would watch creatures of these other worlds for hours, sometimes so oblivious of her surroundings that she didn't notice the rising tide until the waves drenched her.

Her summertime Maine neighbors Dorothy and Stanley Freeman became close friends. She shared picnics with them, sailed in their boat, and sat on her porch with them to enjoy nature's nightly spectacle. Thrilling to the beautiful ocean sunsets, they applauded when the rising moon reflected itself in the waves.

In *The Edge of the Sea,* published in October 1955, Carson "tried to interpret the shore in terms of that essential unity that binds life to the earth." Again she tried to impress upon readers their connection to other forms of life, and the need, therefore, to seek to protect and preserve creatures of the tidelands.

The book marked her development as an ecologist, warning as it did of the dangers of interfering in nature's balance. It concluded with the reflection that the meaning of the teeming life of the shore "haunts and ever eludes us, and in its very pursuit we approach the ultimate mystery of Life itself."

· **TEN** ·

THE EDGE OF THE SEA WAS AN instant success, excerpted in *The New Yorker* and *Reader's Digest* and shooting onto the bestseller list. "It is a truly extraordinary world which Miss Carson vividly unfolds for us," declared the *Atlantic Monthly*, which had had the honor of introducing her work to the public.

Carson now tried to evade claims on her time for speeches and appearances as much as possible. She needed to be let alone to pursue her research, and she also had new family responsibilities. When her niece Marjie died in 1956, Carson took over care of Marjie's little son Roger. At the same time, Carson's mother fell seriously ill with pneumonia, as did Carson herself.

It was a difficult time for her. But personal problems did not prevent Carson from rallying to the defense of the Fish and Wildlife Service when it was attacked by Republican Secretary of the Interior Douglas McKay, who was opening national wildlife refuges to gas and oil leasing.

"A politically minded administration," Carson warned, "returns us to the dark ages of unrestrained exploitation and destruction." Originally uninterested in politics, she began to feel it necessary to support politicians pledged to protect the environment. She worked for Democratic candidate Adlai Stevenson in the 1956 presidential election campaign. With her attention shifting from nature's wonders to man's pollution of them, she also promoted wilderness bills and anti-pollution legislation.

Carson adopted her great-nephew Roger and spent hours introducing him to her wonderful tidelands and the Maine woods, teaching him the names and behaviors of their creatures. Seeing Nature's marvels through a child's eyes once again inspired her to write a magazine article for the *Woman's Home Companion* called "Help Your Child to Wonder." It encouraged parents to share nature with their children, to give them "a sense of the beautiful, the excitement of the new and the unknown." The article was later published in book form under the title *The Sense of Wonder.*

In the summer of 1957, Carson moved into a house built for her in Silver Spring, Maryland, with Roger and her mother. She was grieved to observe the deterioration of her favorite spots at the shore, which she found no longer wild and unspoiled.

"Instead," she wrote in *Holiday* magazine, "they have been cluttered with amusement [areas] . . . refreshment stands, fishing shacks—all the untidy litter of what passes under the name of civilization. . . . On all coasts it is the same. The wild seacoast is vanishing." In the article she proposed turning the coastal shores into parks and wildlife sanctuaries.

Carson's interests took a dramatic turn when she received the letter quoted earlier from her friend Olga Owens Huckins bewailing the loss of songbirds in her neighborhood because of DDT spraying.

"The more I learned about the use of pesticides, the more appalled I became," Carson revealed. In May 1958 she signed with Houghton Mifflin to write *Silent Spring*. She knew her book opposing pesticides would have to be solidly documented to withstand the attacks against it that would be launched by the powerful chemical companies. She thought she could complete the book in one year, but it actually took four because of the need to check, double-check, and triple-check every fact, conferring with hundreds of scientists around the world.

When her mother died in December, Carson was so numbed by grief that for weeks she could not write a word, and was barely able to look after Roger. Utterly worn out, she consulted her doctor, who diagnosed a tumor. Carson underwent an operation to remove it. Feeling weak afterward, she had to engage a secretary to help her with her work and research.

As though she didn't have enough on her hands with the enormous research for *Silent Spring*, Oxford University Press begged her to enlarge and revise *The Sea Around Us* for an updated edition. So Carson worked on both books simultaneously. She added to her earlier book an urgent plea to stop polluting the oceans by dumping radioactive atomic wastes into the sea. Ocean pressure in the depths, she pointed out, could smash open barrels of atomic waste, releasing it into sea waters. "The mistakes made now," she warned, "are made for all time."

· ELEVEN ·

THE DEEPER CARSON DELVED INTO her research, the more she realized it would force her into the limelight she shunned, because the chemical companies were bound to attack her fiercely. The government might also want her silenced for warning the public that it had failed to protect them from the widespread release of dangerous toxins in the environment.

She tried to keep the subject of her new book a secret as long as possible to give herself at least time to marshal the facts.

And the facts she found were startling. Over 600 million pounds of pesticides were produced in the U.S. every year. They were publicized as miracle chemicals that saved farmers' crops and produced more and better fruit and vegetables for consumers. The companies said nothing about the dangers of eating sprayed produce.

In the absence of federal regulation, the manufacture of DDT and other even more toxic pesticides had increased fivefold between 1947 and 1960. Critics charged that the government had turned a blind eye because of the chemical companies' large contributions to political campaign funds.

Carson's struggle to write the book was made even more difficult by what she termed "a whole catalog of illnesses," including flu, arthritis, an eye infection, sinus trouble, an underactive thyroid, and a duodenal ulcer. She wrote a friend wryly, "Somehow I have no wish to read of my ailments in literary gossip columns. Too much comfort to the chemical companies!"

She refused to entertain any notion of letting her ailments force her to give up writing *Silent Spring.* "There would be no peace for me," she explained, "if I kept silent. . . . Knowing the facts as I did, I could not rest."

Inroads on her writing time were also made by the need to attend to her household, look after Roger, and move twice a year between Maryland and her summer home in Maine. In June 1960 the First Lady, Jacqueline Kennedy, asked her to serve on the National Resources Committee of the Democratic Party. She accepted to the limited capacity that her health would permit.

Then in the fall she learned that her tumor had been malignant. She now had to undergo radiation therapy for cancer.

She apologized to her editor, Paul Brooks, explaining that this would necessarily slow up her ability to work on the book.

"But in the intervals," she added, "I hope to work hard and productively. Perhaps even more than ever, I am eager to get the book done." She felt that she had to finish it, in case she might be dying, because of the urgent need to warn that *all* life on earth was in mortal danger from pesticides and pollutants. Even at times when she was bedridden, Carson persisted in writing the book, day after day.

The more she researched her subject, the more alarmed she became that the indiscriminate use of DDT, especially, presented terrible dangers. DDT was sprayed directly on fruit and vegetables destined for markets. Grass and crops sprayed with DDT were eaten by poultry and farm animals. From the fields, DDT leached into rivers that flowed to the sea.

Thus DDT penetrated the food chain of fish, animals, and people—the whole environment. And Carson found that experiments with animals proved that DDT could cause not only cancer but also liver and nerve damage.

When she sent a book chapter on pesticides to a scientist friend for validation, he praised it highly but warned she had better be prepared for a fierce battle with chemical companies.

New Yorker editor William Shawn read the completed manuscript of *Silent Spring*. He phoned Carson late at night to tell her that it was superb and had shocked the living daylights out of him. It would be serialized in *The New Yorker*.

"I knew from his reaction," Carson wrote Dorothy Freeman happily, "that my message would get across. . . . And suddenly the tension of four years was broken and I let the tears come. . . . The thought of all the birds and other creatures and all the loveliness that is in nature came to me with such a surge of deep happiness, that now I had done what I could—I had been able to complete it—now it had its own life."

Almost as soon as the *New Yorker* version appeared in June 1962, shocked readers began sending thousands of furious letters to newspapers, the chemical companies, and the government.

Reprisals against Carson came swiftly from the chemical companies, which allocated a quarter of a million dollars for a public relations campaign to praise the benefits of pesticides. They sought to discredit Carson as a "nature nut," "hysterical bird-watcher" and "food crank" who wanted to turn the earth over to the insects.

"One obvious way to try to weaken a cause," Carson replied in a December 1962 speech to the Women's National Press Club, "is to discredit the person who champions it."

The Department of Agriculture, siding with the chemical companies and agribusiness, also argued against Carson's conclusions. Her publisher was told that she was a pawn being used by "sinister influences to cripple U.S. food production to reduce it to Communist levels."

· **TWELVE** ·

PRESIDENT JOHN F. KENNEDY created a special panel of his Science Advisory Committee, consisting of leading scientists, to investigate Carson's findings. Their report completely vindicated her. "Until the publication of *Silent Spring* by Rachel Carson," it declared, "people were generally unaware of the toxicity of pesticides."

Congressional hearings were quickly announced to consider new bills to limit the chemical pollution Carson had revealed. On Capitol Hill, Senator William Proxmire of Wisconsin and Representative John V. Lindsay of New York read parts of *Silent Spring* into the *Congressional Record.*

"A great woman," declared Secretary of the Interior Stewart Udall, "has awakened the Nation by her forceful account of the danger around us. We owe much to Rachel Carson."

When the book was published in September 1962, reviewers praised it enthusiastically. All agreed that Carson had proved the need for much greater care in the use of pesticides to protect both the public and the environment.

With all this uproar, *Silent Spring* sold half a million copies and remained on the *New York Times* best-seller list for more than half a year. It garnered eight awards and was published in dozens of countries. CBS TV broadcast *The Silent Spring of Rachel Carson,* ignoring strong pressure from sponsors to keep the documentary off the air.

Despite her illness, Carson courageously agreed to defend her book against her attackers by appearing on TV, making speeches, giving newspaper and magazine interviews, and attending luncheons and receptions in her honor.

"Anyone who has really read the book," she declared, "knows that I criticize the modern chemical method not because it *controls* harmful insects but because it controls them *badly* and *inefficiently* and creates many dangerous side effects in doing so."

As for the furor she had aroused, Carson wrote to a friend, "The beauty of the living world I was trying to save has always been uppermost in my mind—that, and anger at the senseless, brutish things that were being done. . . . Now I can believe I have at least helped a little."

There is little doubt that *Silent Spring* deserves credit for initiating the modern environmental movement. It brought about reform by changing the direction of people's thinking about the world they live in. Carson's book also influenced the government to establish the Environmental Protection Agency in 1970 and compelled the EPA to correct the problems she had pointed out.

Thoroughly worn out and weakened by her painful cancer, Carson continued to crusade in person for her cause, even when she could scarcely walk. She told Dorothy Freeman that her health was a war she knew she would lose in the long run. "But—one battle at a time. I intend to win as many as I can."

In May and June 1963, a subcommittee of the Senate Committee on Government Operations began a two-year investigation to determine how government agencies could cooperate to prevent and reduce pesticide use and all kinds of pollution. Carson agreed to testify on behalf of two bills introduced by Oregon Senator Maureen B. Neuberger. One required the Department of Agriculture to consult with the Department of the Interior before authorizing pesticide programs. The other required containers of pesticides harmful to fish and wildlife to be so labeled.

"Miss Carson," Connecticut Senator Abraham Ribicoff greeted her, "on behalf of the committee, we certainly welcome you here. You are the lady who started all this. . . . All people in this country and around the world owe you a debt of gratitude for your writings and for your actions toward making the atmosphere and the environment safe for habitation."

Carson proposed the creation of a Pesticide Commission to be "made up of citizens of high professional competence in such fields as medicine, genetics, biology, and conservation . . . [to] bring about far greater safety and sanity in the handling of pesticides, for the benefit not only of wildlife but of mankind."

She added, "My feeling is not that we must never use pesticides, but I think we must use them selectively and sparingly, and we must, as rapidly as possible, develop less toxic materials. . . . I think at the present time and in the past there has been too little to warn the consumer that he is buying and using a very hazardous substance."

The registration of chemicals, she urged, should not be up to the Secretary of Agriculture alone, but should also involve the Department of Health, Education and Welfare, the Department of the Interior, and the Fish and Wildlife Service.

Carson also called for research to find out whether the pesticide chemicals in the concentrations in which they were being used, or at the levels to which they could build up in the human body, were capable of causing cancer and other illnesses.

"Miss Carson," Alaska Senator Ernest Gruening told her, "every once in a while in the history of mankind a book has appeared which has substantially altered the course of history. . . . Your book is of that important character, and I feel you have rendered a tremendous service."

· **THIRTEEN** ·

IN THE FALL OF 1963 MARIE RODELL helped Carson make a trip to the Sierra Club in San Francisco. She was thrilled with a tour of the giant California redwoods and the Muir Woods. In December she traveled to New York to be elected one of just fifty members of the American Academy of Arts and Letters. She was guest of honor at an American Geographic Society reception, and was also awarded an Audubon Society medal for achievement in conservation. By now, Carson spent most of her time in a wheelchair, and could walk only with a cane.

At the end of February 1964, she needed to undergo another operation, after which she required bed rest under a nurse's care. She wrote Dorothy Freeman, "Now every month, every day, is precious."

Freeman, who had recently lost her husband, came to stay with Carson in Silver Spring and to look after Roger for her. She fought back tears when Carson told her she was happy in knowing that "it is a natural and not unhappy thing that a life comes to an end."

One night early in April 1964, Carson asked the attending nurse to wake her before dawn next morning. The sun had not yet risen when she was wheeled out into her yard and left there, at her request. As the first yellow rays cut through the night clouds, she listened intently. Then she heard them. All the beautiful bird melodies, sung as though in a grateful farewell tribute to their good friend, Rachel Carson.

It was the last time she would hear their dawn songs. On April 14, 1964, at age 56, her heart finally gave out. At her funeral the final passage from *The Edge of the Sea* was read aloud, at her request. Her will disclosed that she had left her estate to her family, the Sierra Club, and the Nature Conservancy.

Eventually all twelve of the most toxic agents she had exposed in *Silent Spring*, including DDT, were banned or restricted. Twelve years after her death, the Toxic Substances Act of 1976 further tightened federal controls over abuses she had described.

Her books about the sea continue to be read and loved by millions, raising their consciousness about nature and the need to preserve our heritage of wildlife and ocean creatures.

Like John Muir, Rachel Carson had sought to reacquaint city dwellers with the outdoor world they were losing. "Most of us," she wrote, "walk unseeing through the world, unaware of its beauties, its wonders, and the strange and sometimes terrible intensity of the lives that are being lived around us."

But it was for her valiant and victorious crusade against chemical pollution and calling for the protection of all living creatures, including ourselves, from its poisons that Rachel Carson will long be remembered in history.

David McTaggart, 1981.
(© Greenpeace, 1981)

David McTaggart

of Greenpeace

1 9 3 2 –

"It's Everybody's Planet!"

· ONE ·

WHEN SOFT-SPOKEN DAVID MCTAGGART, thirty-nine, bought an old thirty-eight-foot sailboat, the *Vega*, he planned to spend the rest of his life sailing the South Seas. Instead he became the leader of a dynamic international environmental movement that challenged any government that polluted the earth.

It all began in Auckland, New Zealand, in 1972, when McTaggart became incensed by a newspaper report. The French Navy had announced its intention to set off a huge nuclear test explosion in the atmosphere over the French colony at Mururoa atoll. In violation of international law, the French banned all shipping in 100,000 square miles of the Pacific in the path of radioactive fallout.

"What angered me about the atomic bomb tests," McTaggart told me, "was the fact that the French government simply said, 'We forbid anyone to travel through this area, because we are testing our bomb.' No government has the right to control the free and open ocean for any reason, and this made me really mad. Here I was in the one place left on earth, the ocean, where there are no nations, no borders, and no government, and someone was telling me I could not sail there."

McTaggart determined to challenge the French ban by sailing the *Vega* into the forbidden zone to block the nuclear tests. His action was inspired by a small Quaker group in Vancouver, Canada, called the "Don't Make a Wave Committee." Fearing that planned United States atomic bomb tests in the Aleutians might trigger an earthquake that could cause tidal waves, the Quakers had sought to stop the tests by sailing into the test zone.

Similarly, McTaggart now gambled his life to stop the French atomic test. The danger was threefold. The French might sink the *Vega*. If they went ahead with the test, despite the *Vega*'s presence, the blast might blow McTaggart and his crew of volunteers to pieces. Or the radioactive fallout could poison them fatally.

In the name of humanity, they sailed for Mururoa.

David McTaggart was born in Vancouver in 1932. He developed a love of nature as a child during summer vacations on beautiful Buccaneer Bay, a paradise of water holes, trees, and mountains. A superb athlete, David was a fifteen-year-old unknown when he walked into the Vancouver Lawn and Tennis Club and won five of their six junior championships. He upset many of the very reserved British members by his fierce determination to win.

"It was terribly crude to try too hard," he recalled in amusement, "and I had tried much too hard."

At eighteen he challenged the senior Canadian badminton champion and defeated him. At twenty-three he played the U.S. badminton champion, Joe Alison, and beat him for the Thomas Cup. He then went on to challenge the world champion, and beat him as well.

While lining up sports trophies, David was also working full-time. At fifteen he spent the first of two summers prospecting for gold in the Rocky Mountains. At eighteen David wandered to Montana and worked in a corn processing factory. At nineteen he took a job as a laborer and time-keeper for a construction outfit. By the time he was twenty-two, he had started his own construction company, which he ran for the next seventeen years, until it failed.

McTaggart next became general manager and vice-president of the four-hundred-acre Bear Valley Ski Resort in the High Sierras east of San Francisco. Happily married by this time to his wife Betty and the doting father of three children, McTaggart combined business with pleasure by joining his family on the slopes.

One afternoon in 1968 a propane tank exploded in the ski lodge, destroying it and badly injuring two employees. Shocked and appalled, McTaggart lost all interest in pursuing a business career. "My drive for upward mobility," he said later, "had ended that afternoon in the High Sierras."

He lost a lawsuit against the propane company. At the same time, his marriage began to come apart. Disheartened, McTaggart decided to make a fresh start in a remote part of the world. In 1969, he gave his Mercedes to a friend, left home, and escaped to Tahiti.

Here he stayed with an artist friend, "drinking myself hopefully into oblivion." After six months he had worked through his depression and felt an urge to go to sea. He left for New Zealand to find a cheap ketch to sail in.

"I had been raised on the ocean," he told me, "and I had always wanted to sail the Pacific. The ocean is someplace where you are truly free."

In Auckland he bought the *Vega* and met and fell in love with a New Zealander, Ann-Marie Horne. When he decided to make the dangerous voyage to Mururoa, her father Gene volunteered to sail with him. A twenty-six-year-old British navigator, Nigel Ingram, also offered to join him in defying France.

The Department of Law at Auckland University armed McTaggart with a letter certifying that France had no legal right to ban anyone from the Pacific's international waters. He and his crew worked furiously to get the *Vega* shipshape in time for them to reach Mururoa before the French tests were scheduled.

"Like every reasonable person," McTaggart said later, "I was against nuclear weapons and their testing, but I had never before protested against anything." Now he felt that someone had to risk a stand against poisoning of the atmosphere and the sea. And he was in a position to do it.

· T W O ·

TEN YEARS EARLIER, IN 1962, France had selected its Polynesian colonies in the Pacific as nuclear test sites, despite protests from the islanders. The tiny atoll of Mururoa, seven hundred miles southeast of Tahiti, had been chosen as a prime test site, after the inhabitants had been taken off the island.

After the first successful test there, Prime Minister Charles de Gaulle planned to witness the next explosion, scheduled for September 19, 1966, from a French cruiser. But the test was postponed because the wind was blowing westward toward some inhabited islands. Next day it continued to blow westward, and de Gaulle grew impatient. He ordered the bomb detonated anyway.

Political commentators suggested that de Gaulle's reckless enthusiasm for exploding nuclear weapons reflected embarrassment over France's rapid defeat in World War II by Germany, and the belief that blowing up the big bombs would reestablish France as a major power in the eyes of the superpowers.

New Zealand monitoring stations reported heavy radioactive fallout from the test in the Cook Islands, Niue, Samoa, Tonga, Fiji, and Tuvala. One researcher, Dr. Tilman A. Ruff, found instances of fish poisoning in the Micronesia islands as a result of radiation of the coral reefs by the atomic tests. Significantly, the French government stopped publishing health statistics of French Polynesians once their testing program had begun.

That was the situation in 1972 when McTaggart and his volunteers determined to block the new French tests at Mururoa. He knew no one in the Don't Make a Wave Committee, but sent his brother in Vancouver to ask them for financial help with the *Vega*'s mission. "They offered to buy a radio set, which I naturally accepted," McTaggart told me. "That cost around $2,500 and that was the only funding I was given to make the trip by the Vancouver group."

Nevertheless, because the Don't Make a Wave Committee had launched two small boats for protests called *Greenpeace I* and *II*, McTaggart had the name *Greenpeace III* stitched to the *Vega*'s mainsail and painted on its stern.

The French sought to avoid further international embarrassment by preventing McTaggart from sailing. A newspaper report revealed that they had warned the New Zealand government that, if the *Vega* was allowed to embark from Auckland for the forbidden test zone, France might have to reconsider its large purchases of New Zealand butter.

On April 18, 1972, the day before McTaggart's scheduled departure, five plainclothes police suddenly showed up at the *Vega*'s berth. They claimed to have a search warrant but refused to let McTaggart see it. They swarmed onto the boat and made a shambles of everything they touched. McTaggart and Ingram were searched roughly. Two customs officers in uniform followed the police aboard. Citing an infraction of customs regulations, they ordered McTaggart to report to the station house the following morning.

When McTaggart appeared in court, he was found guilty of a customs violation. Fined eight hundred dollars or sentenced to 120 days in prison, he was jailed until the fine was paid for him. Almost immediately after his release, a marine department inspector appeared at the *Vega*, insisting the sailboat would have to pass a safety survey before it could leave. Another week's delay.

But if the *Vega* was not at sea within two days, McTaggart

doubted that he could reach Mururoa before the French tests began. And he was wryly aware that the "survey" could concoct reasons to delay the departure of the *Vega* indefinitely.

As though that were not enough to hold him in port, another policeman appeared and ordered McTaggart to report to the police station the next morning to "talk about some immigration forms" that he allegedly had failed to fill out. That was the morning of his scheduled departure.

McTaggart pretended to consent, but he had absolutely no intention of showing up. He had had enough! He and Nigel Ingram worked frantically to load the last food and supplies.

Early next morning, loading completed, McTaggart started the *Vega*'s engines. He awaited only the momentary arrival of Gene Horne, who suddenly appeared at the wharf out of breath. He panted that the immigration department was delaying his passport for a week. McTaggart made a hasty phone call and succeeded in enlisting a last-minute replacement—a New Zealand/Australian dual citizen, Grant Davidson, who had asked to go along.

Several dozen New Zealanders who knew of McTaggart's departure date came down to the shore to see them off. He, Ingram, and Davidson waved good-bye as car headlights flashed on and off and horns honked. The *Vega* was off on its perilous voyage at last.

· **THREE** ·

FOR FORTY-THREE DAYS THE LITTLE *Vega* battled fierce winds and high seas. After sailing 3,500 miles, on June 1, 1972, it finally breached the area banned by the French. McTaggart set a course twenty miles downwind of the atoll. Here they would not be within the twelve-mile limit of the ocean officially controlled by Mururoa, so the French could not legally arrest them. But if the French went ahead with their nuclear explosion, the blast would smother them in deadly radiation.

"When I arrived at a point thirteen miles off Mururoa," McTaggart told me, "I informed the French that I was in international waters, that they had no right to interfere with my sailing there, and that I was staying."

Attempting to hold position, the trio had to fight the constant rolling of the ship in high seas. French planes and a helicopter suddenly appeared, buzzing the *Vega* and tossing it in the wind-whipped waves. McTaggart sought to report his position by marine radio, only to discover that the French were jamming his transmissions.

Switching to the sloop's emergency frequency, he finally reached a man identifying himself as a radio operator named Mueller on a Belgian ship eight hundred miles distant. Relieved, McTaggart sent Mueller daily updates on his situation for relay to media around the world. What McTaggart didn't know was that "Mueller" was actually a radio operator on the French cruiser *De Grasse* that was keeping them under observation from a distance.

Through binoculars, on June 16 McTaggart watched a French balloon lift a huge nuclear bomb above the atoll. He radioed at once, "Balloon raised over Mururoa. . . . *Greenpeace III* 16 miles northeast. Situation frightening. Please pray."

His message never left the *De Grasse.*

McTaggart's pulse raced. But he and his crew grimly set about challenging the French even more defiantly. Hoisting sail, they moved even closer to the target area, where the bomb explosion would certainly bring an instant and horrible death.

Next morning a French navy minesweeper suddenly hove into view a mile off the *Vega*'s port bow. Its captain dispatched an inflatable boat called a Zodiac to warn the protestors formally that the tests would begin shortly. McTaggart was or-

The vessel Greenpeace III *heading for Mururoa to*
stop French nuclear tests, 1972.
(Photo courtesy Greenpeace)

dered to leave the danger zone at once. Refusing, he defiantly
handed the French his Auckland University Law Department
letter affirming his legal right to remain where he was.

At dawn the next day, he and his two crewmen were awakened when the huge French cruiser *De Grasse* sped past and
cut across their bow. Ingram quickly started the *Vega*'s engine
and swung the ketch to port. A collision was averted by just
ten yards.

On both sides of the *Vega*, two French minesweepers now

closed in, boxing the little ship in dangerously high sea swells as they sped back and forth.

"They had broken the most basic law of the seas," McTaggart said afterwards, "which is not to block the path of another vessel under sail." But the French were still not through harassing them. A twin-engined plane roared over the *Vega* close to mast level, adding to the sailboat's perilous pitching and tossing as the pilot kept circling above. McTaggart had to shout at his crewmen to be heard as they struggled to keep the *Vega* from overturning.

The minesweepers sped by, narrowly missing them.

"The French had gone crazy!" McTaggart sighed. "Undoubtedly with orders to scare the hell out of us, they'd become inflamed and were vying with one another in their recklessness."

Abruptly, after more than an hour of these attacks, the minesweepers retreated and the plane flew off. The reason, McTaggart learned later, was that the French had by now tested the trigger mechanism of the bomb, although not the bomb itself. The harassment and noise of the plane had been intended to mask the sound of the blast.

On June 30 McTaggart was outraged to hear over the *Vega*'s radio a Radio Australia newscast declaring, "The French government has informed Canada that the Canadian peace vessel *Greenpeace III* sailed away from the Pacific nuclear test area June 21 and has not been seen since. . . . *Greenpeace III* was not intercepted and sailed away on its own initiative."

The French were putting out the story that they had left the test area *nine days earlier!*

"David, that can only mean one thing," Ingram exclaimed grimly. "They intend to sink us!"

McTaggart, too, was convinced that the French intended to

send the *Vega* to the bottom with impunity. He and his crew would simply be reported as "lost at sea."

Next morning the French minesweeper *La Paimpolaise* reappeared and circled the *Vega*. Then it swerved and headed for the sailboat's starboard bow on a collision course. Ingram swung the wheel over sharply to veer away. But the bow of the minesweeper crashed into the side of the wooden ship, entangling the rigging and dragging it along. To free the *Vega*, McTaggart swiftly chopped off the rigging.

He took a quick inventory of the damage. The *Vega* was now leaking severely and in bad shape, certainly unable to make the nearest neutral port. Raising a distress flag, he set off two distress flares.

· F O U R ·

CAPTAIN ROCHEBROCHARD OF *La Paimpolaise* and two seamen approached the crippled ship in a Zodiac.

Boarding the *Vega*, he told McTaggart apologetically, "I'm sorry, I'm sorry. What do you wish me to do?"

McTaggart angrily demanded that the collision and his position be reported at once to the American, Canadian, Australian, and New Zealand governments, and that the *Vega* be escorted to a port for repairs. He also insisted upon hearing a confirmation of the cabled messages from New Zealand and Australia.

The minesweeper captain shook his head. French Admiral Claverlie at Mururoa, he murmured, would simply not permit such a cable to be sent.

"If not," McTaggart flared, "we will radio a Mayday that will bring out air-sea rescue from the New Zealand air force. We dare not turn ourselves over to you until our governments know where we are!"

It was a desperate bluff. McTaggart knew that the French could see that his radio aerial had been smashed in the collision. But Rochebrochard simply shrugged and returned to his minesweeper. Meanwhile, the *Vega* drifted helplessly toward the atoll. When it crossed the twelve-mile limit, McTaggart knew, the French would be able to arrest him and his two crewmen legally.

In a little while Rochebrochard returned with an invitation for McTaggart, Ingram, and Davidson to board the minesweeper, and communicate by radio with Admiral Claverlie.

When they did so, the French admiral flatly refused McTaggart's demand that his message be relayed. However, Claverlie purred, if McTaggart would sign a written request, the *Vega* would be towed into Mururoa for repairs, after which he and his crew would be allowed to sail her away.

McTaggart had no choice. The *Vega* was in no shape to sail off on her own. And the French could make both ship and crew disappear, with no one the wiser as to what had happened. He signed the request, and the *Vega* was towed in.

While the *Vega* was being repaired, Admiral Claverlie invited the three environmentalists to swim in the atoll's lagoon. Suspicious of this sudden hospitality, McTaggart spotted a photographer with a telephoto lens hiding behind a tree. The French, he realized, were setting them up, hoping to photograph them swimming in the lagoon. Released to the world's press, such photos would indicate that the *Vega*'s crew considered the atoll's waters radiation-free, belittling the danger of the nuclear tests.

McTaggart refused the invitation. However, after weeks of tinned and dried food aboard the *Vega,* he and his crew were irresistibly tempted by an invitation to a superb French lunch with the admiral.

McTaggart found the admiral charismatic, subtle, and very

amiable. Claverlie claimed not to know anything about the false report that the *Vega* had left Mururoa ten days earlier. He promised to ask Paris for approval to report to the news media that the three environmentalists were still at the atoll.

Meanwhile, French photographers using telephoto lenses were recording the lunch. These photos were distributed to world media to discredit McTaggart's claim that he and his crew had been persecuted by the French.

The media was told by the French that the *Vega* had "made a mistake in manoeuvering," and had crashed into a French minesweeper. The French had "generously responded to the *Vega*'s plea for help." And Admiral Claverlie had invited the crew to a fine lunch with him. Later, McTaggart realized unhappily that the French had outmaneuvered him in public relations, cancelling the impact of his first voyage of protest.

Subsequently France's Minister of Overseas Territories admitted that the French secret service, the *Direction Générale de la Sécurité Expérieure* (DGSE), had been plotting actions against anti-nuclear protesters who threatened France's atomic tests.

McTaggart told Jim Bohlen, a leading activist in Canada's Don't Make a Wave Committee, that he planned to sue France for the damage done to the *Vega*. He asked Bohlen to help.

"There was no real Greenpeace organization then," McTaggart said later. "It was still the Don't Make a Wave Committee. Bohlen and his friend said they couldn't help; court cases were too long and drawn out. . . . So I set up a bank account in north Vancouver in the name of Greenpeace. I think it was the first account set up in that name. I raised a little money and went to Paris with about two hundred dollars to start the case. I . . . wrote about thirty letters a day back to Canada to build a pressure base on the Canadian government.

In the meantime, people in Europe were pushing me to start a Greenpeace office there."

When Bohlen's movement became Greenpeace Canada, mismanagement piled up a $300,000 debt. "The Canadian organization sued the U.S. Greenpeace [over the use of the name]," McTaggart told me, "in order to try to pay off that debt. But they did not own the rights [to the name]. . . . There are many different stories about how the name Greenpeace came about. All anyone seems to agree is that it was 1971 when it started popping up all over."

McTaggart began Greenpeace Europe with himself as chairman, opening an office in Paris, then in London and Amsterdam. "I negotiated a settlement between the U.S. and Canadian units," he told me, "and Greenpeace Europe paid off that debt."

In 1973 the French ignored protests and planned a new series of atomic tests at Mururoa. When McTaggart promptly announced another voyage to try to block them, the French government offered to pay him five thousand dollars for the damage to the *Vega* if he called off his lawsuit as well as his new protest voyage.

"The notice was made through the Ministry of Foreign Affairs in Ottawa," McTaggart told me. "The costs [of *Vega* damage] were in excess of $13,000. I told them to take a walk. . . . Perhaps more than any other single thing, that confirmed in my mind the decision to get rolling!"

· FIVE ·

MCTAGGART SAILED THE *VEGA* out of Auckland on July 9, 1973, with his girlfriend Ann-Marie Horne, Nigel Ingram, and Ingram's girlfriend Mary Lornie. McTaggart hoped that the presence of the two women would make the French hesitate before ramming the *Vega* again.

Foul weather kept them locked at anchor just off the New Zealand coast for thirteen days, before fair weather and a strong wind sent them sailing for Mururoa. The delay let the French test two atom bombs with no interference from McTaggart. He crossed into the test area on August 12, ahead of a third planned test, and let the French Navy know they had arrived.

On the day scheduled for the test they were only thirty-five miles from Mururoa when the French minesweeper *La Dunkerquoise* approached the ketch's stern at full speed. It dropped an inflatable Zodiac with four men who approached the *Vega*. McTaggart filmed them with his movie camera.

As the raft came alongside, a French lieutenant handed McTaggart an envelope. McTaggart handed him one with the University of Auckland letter certifying the *Vega*'s right to be there. After reading it, the French lieutenant disdainfully flung it back onto the deck of the *Vega*. McTaggart threw it back to him. The document went back and forth until the French officer finally flung it into the sea and returned his Zodiac to the minesweeper.

Inside the envelope he had handed to McTaggart was an order to leave at once, because the declared zone of exclusion was now legal under French law—though not under international law. Ignoring the French demand, McTaggart kept the *Vega* on course for Mururoa. He planned to stop just one mile short of the twelve-mile territorial limit, so the *Vega* would remain in international waters.

Suddenly *La Dunkerquoise* came racing back toward their stern at full speed, heading for a collision. They all braced for impact. Just before smashing into the *Vega*, the minesweeper swerved away. A few minutes later it repeated the threat, this time not changing course until almost on top of the rocking *Vega*.

Two more French Navy ships headed for them from Mururoa. One towed a Zodiac with sailors. McTaggart tried to steer the *Vega* away. But the sailors pulled up alongside, grabbed the sloop's rail, and leaped onto its deck.

"This is private property!" McTaggart roared. "You can't come aboard!"

The sailors attacked him with clubs.

"The first truncheon came down with a weight and force unlike anything I had ever felt on the back of my head," he related later, "and the second came down across my shoulders, and the next blow landed on the back of my neck, and the next on my head again, and the next on my spine, and the next on my shoulder blade, and the next against my kidney . . . as though they all had gone mad and were simply trying to smash me to death, stamp me out of existence like some loathsome bug. . . . Something crashed into my right eye with such incredible force that it seemed to come right into the middle of my brain in an explosion. . . . And then everything went black."

Knocked unconscious, with serious damage to his kidneys, spine, and head, and temporary blindness in one eye, McTaggart was carried onto the Zodiac. Even here the French sailors continued to rain blows down on the *Vega* skipper.

The sailors also seized Nigel Ingram, and clubbed and kicked him savagely in the stomach, groin, and ribs until he, too, blacked out. Mary Lornie recorded the beatings with McTaggart's movie camera, but a French sailor seized it and threw it overboard.

Luckily, Ann-Marie Horne had also been filming on a 35-millimeter camera. She sprang down the forward hatch and locked the door behind her. She was able to shove the camera into a hiding place just before the door burst open and she was dragged back on deck.

The boarding party took control of the *Vega* and steered it into Mururoa harbor. When the *Vega* moored, the French sailors jumped ashore briefly to dock the sloop. Ingram, Horne, and Lornie quickly dashed into the cabin below and locked the hatchway. Horne retrieved the camera from its hiding place and removed the film. Knocking loudly and insistently, the French soldiers demanded that the three disembark. Ingram shouted in French that they were getting some personal belongings and would be up in a minute.

Worried about being searched, Horne secreted the film in her body. Then they opened the hatch, and were taken ashore to be flown out of the test zone.

· SIX ·

MCTAGGART, MEANWHILE, HAD been transferred from the Zodiac to *La Dunkerquoise*. His injuries were examined and found to be extremely serious, especially damage to his eye. He was flown to a French hospital in Tahiti against his wishes. Fearing that his life was still in jeopardy, he repeatedly refused any treatment until he could call his brother Drew. "I suspected the syringe was meant to immobilize or kill me," McTaggart told me.

The French doctors warned that McTaggart would go blind unless his eye was treated at once. But they finally threw up their hands and let him place a call to his brother. He told Drew where he was and what had happened. Then he instructed his brother to wire the Canadian Prime Minister, Pierre Trudeau, to ask the French for his immediate release and the release of the others on the *Vega*.

Drew McTaggart vowed to do it at once. Then he urged, "Let them treat you right away! For God's sake, don't push it any longer!" McTaggart finally consented to an operation.

His eye was saved. Twelve days later he was flown to Vancouver, where he was greeted by his brother Drew and Ingram. They told him that Horne and Lornie had been flown back to New Zealand, and about the storm that Horne's photos had stirred up in Canada when Drew passed the film along to Greenpeace.

The French Naval High Command insisted that their sailors had not attacked the *Vega*'s crew, but that McTaggart had injured himself when he slipped on deck. The pictures, published in over twenty countries—though banned in France—revealed the lie.

McTaggart urged the Canadian government to pursue the case with the French government. But Prime Minister Trudeau was reluctant to disturb French-Canadian relations, despite the public's show of support for McTaggart.

"The Canadian government," McTaggart told me, "was too involved in uranium deals with the French to back me up." Ottawa obliged Paris by refusing to support his lawsuit against the French government. McTaggart learned that even *before* the *Vega* had been attacked, Admiral Claverlie had received assurances from Ottawa that Canada would not make an issue of it.

McTaggart was advised by the Canadian government to sue the French in their own courts. He did so, and eventually won a verdict that held the French Navy minesweeper *La Paimpolaise* guilty of ramming the *Vega*. The French Navy was ordered to pay McTaggart damages.

Meanwhile the New Zealand government was getting increasingly disturbed by France's atomic tests in the atmosphere in the South Pacific. It filed a successful lawsuit to stop them in the International Court of Justice at the Hague. In 1975 France then resorted to testing the weapons underground.

Reporters asked McTaggart if he was satisfied with this concession by the French. He replied that they were probably lying, and that in any case the new tests would also explode the more deadly neutron bombs. Besides, how dared they continue to endanger the lives of South Pacific islanders by blasting such terrible weapons?

· SEVEN ·

THE FRENCH WROTE MCTAGGART that he could have the *Vega* back if he sailed her away immediately. But the Canadian doctors who had treated his permanently impaired eye warned that he could not undertake any long voyage now, because he would need to be within fourteen hours of ophthalmological help.

Greenpeace sympathizers flooded the Canadian government with protests. Ottawa finally agreed to pay twelve thousand dollars to have the *Vega* shipped on a freighter to Vancouver. McTaggart urged the Canadian government to demand reimbursement from France.

By 1975 Greenpeace membership had increased to ten thousand, and McTaggart had acquired a small chartered or loaned "econavy." Now the organization could expand its activities to include the protection of sea creatures, along with continuing anti-nuclear protests. They first targeted the killing of whales, which Russian and Japanese fleets were slaughtering indiscriminately, in violation of internationally accepted quotas.

Greenpeace crews set sail in the *Vega* and the *Phyllis Mc-Cormack* to patrol whaling waters. McTaggart arranged for both to carry inflatable Zodiacs, the small, highly maneuverable ships which the French had used against the *Vega*. When the *Phyllis McCormack* came upon the Russian factory ship

Dalniy Vostok and a whaling fleet off California, the Green-peacers took off in Zodiacs and positioned themselves be-tween the harpoon guns and the whales. The harpooners first pointed their guns menacingly at the Zodiacs, but then fired at the whales, scoring hits that turned the sea crimson.

When the Zodiacs persisted in staying in the line of fire, the Russian captain of the *Dalniy Vostok* abandoned the hunt. He was unaware that the confrontation had been filmed by a Greenpeace cameraman aboard the *Phyllis McCormack.* Re-leased to TV, the film's broadcast infuriated millions of North Americans.

Greenpeacers next followed icebreakers in a trawler to the ice floes off Labrador and Newfoundland, the site of the annual Canadian and Norwegian seal hunt. Greenpeacers placed their bodies between packs of baby seals and hunters' clubs, risking attack, arrest, or a plunge into the icy seas. An-other tactic was to spray baby seals with an indelible green dye. This made their pelts worthless to furriers, so the seals were not worth killing.

McTaggart knew well how much public support could be won by using the media. Filming attacks on whales, dolphins, and seals became a powerful tool of Greenpeace crusades. Pictures of the seal slaughter, faxed around the world, created such intense protest that the slaughter of Canadian seals dropped from 204,000 in 1981 to only 5,401 in 1985, the smallest hunt in Canada's two-hundred-year history of com-mercial sealing.

"We are nonviolent and nonpolitical," McTaggart ex-plained. "We have and will continue to take on every excess of the military-governmental-industrial hierarchy . . . even if we have to break trespass laws to do it. What the hell, it's everybody's planet!"

In 1978 McTaggart arranged for the purchase of an old North Sea cod trawler in England, the first big ship actually owned by Greenpeace. He christened it the *Rainbow Warrior*, after an Indian legend that predicted a time when birds, fish, and deer would die, and the seas grow black, because of man's greed. At that point the Indians would teach the white man to have reverence for the sacred earth, and all the world's races would unite under the symbol of the rainbow. As "warriors of the Rainbow," the Greenpeacers would seek to end man's destruction of his environment and of his fellow creatures sharing the earth.

McTaggart sailed on the maiden voyage of the *Rainbow Warrior*, the first of many he would join. He was on board in July 1978 when the *Warrior* tried to block the dumping of two thousand tons of low-level radioactive waste in the ocean by the British transport ship *GEM*. He had trained the *Warrior* crew how to use the Zodiacs. They positioned the crafts directly beneath the *GEM*'s dumping platform. That did not stop the *GEM*'s crew from dumping seven-hundred-pound cylinders of nuclear waste overboard. One hit a Zodiac a glancing blow. Greenpeace film of this incident provoked an angry outcry in England.

Greenpeace activist Peter Wilkinson described what the mission was like: "Theorizing about how to stop three-ton barrels of waste being tipped into the ocean from a moving ship is one thing, but when it's time to put those theories in practice, the results can be summed up in one word: terrifying. You are faced with an impersonal wall of steel, massive bow waves, high pressure hoses, noise, screamed obscenities, chaos, and danger. You brace your back instinctively and wonder what the hell you're doing there."

· EIGHT ·

MCTAGGART'S NEXT TARGET WAS Icelandic whalers. The crew of the *Rainbow Warrior* chased the whaling ships, interposing their Zodiacs between the whales and the harpoons. When the exploding harpoons found their targets, Greenpeacers photographed the slaughter. They kept the pressure up for more than six weeks—despite the fact that the Icelandic government had issued an order for their arrest, and sent a warship out to deliver it!

In September the *Warrior* sailed for the Scottish Orkney Islands, where the Greenpeacers staged a nine-day protest against a Norwegian sealing ship, preventing the slaughter of four thousand gray seals. The publicity they won induced Scotland to ban seal hunting in the Orkney Islands.

Despite their successes in the field, friction erupted in 1979 among Greenpeace's international branches over internal organization. Angry lawsuits were filed and McTaggart had to fly in from London to act as a peacemaker.

"There were arguments," he explained later, "but we made the difficult decision to unite under one set of campaigns, one set of policies, and one name. The transition was remarkable. What had been a bunch of people trying to rock a boat by jumping up and down at different times suddenly started to coordinate what they were doing. That was when we really started making waves." McTaggart united the Canadian, United States, New Zealand, and Australian chapters with Greenpeace Europe. The new organization was called Greenpeace International. A fifteen-member world council elected McTaggart as chairman.

In addition to fighting to save whales and seals, McTaggart was concerned by the slaughter of dolphins inadvertently trapped in tuna nets, especially by Japan. A Greenpeace International contingent was sent to Japan to protest in 1978. They were able to stop the killing temporarily by proving that Japan's pollution of the sea with industrial mercury wastes had made the dolphins poisonous.

In January 1980 the *Warrior* tried to block a Japanese freighter carrying radioactive spent nuclear fuel rods from entering the harbor of Cherbourg, France. A French cruiser warned the Greenpeacers off, and two French tugs and a minesweeper blocked the *Warrior*'s path. Fifty French riot police boarded and seized control of the Greenpeace ship.

The freighter was able to unload its fuel rods at the dock, but French Greenpeacers blocked a train waiting to transport them to the reprocessing plant near Cherbourg. Riot police dispersed the local Greenpeacers with high-pressure hoses.

Next day the French Navy forced the *Warrior* out of French waters, banning it from ever returning. But French Navy officials were furious when they read the headline in a French paper the next day: GREENPEACE MAKES FOOLS OF FRENCH NAVY.

This new frustration, on top of their humiliation by McTaggart in the South Pacific, only increased the French Navy's fierce hostility toward him and all Greenpeace activists. That hostility was soon to have dramatic and disastrous consequences for McTaggart.

· NINE ·

IN JUNE 1980 THE *WARRIOR* SAILED into Spanish waters again to stop whale killing. The *Warrior* represented nine countries and millions of people who appealed to the whaler to stop its slaughter. But the crew's actions to protect the whales were cut short by the arrival of two Spanish corvettes. Despite the fact that the *Warrior* was in international waters, the crew of one corvette boarded the ship and forced it into a Spanish naval base.

The *Warrior* and its crew were held captive for five months by Spain. Meanwhile, film which had been secretly made of the *Warrior*'s capture was smuggled out and broadcast in more than seventy countries, enraging Spanish authorities. When sympathizers from Spain sought to demonstrate in support of the release of the Greenpeacers and their ship, they were attacked with batons by Spanish police. The Greenpeacers were not released, but they managed to escape.

"I smuggled my way on board [the *Warrior*] the day before we escaped," McTaggart told me. Observing that the Spanish guards on the ship had slipped off to a party, he told the crew, "This is it!" Pulling up anchor, they sped off and were long gone by the time the frantic Spanish dispatched two warships and Navy helicopters to try to track them down.

This would be McTaggart's last voyage as captain of the *Warrior*. With the *Warrior* in serious need of repair, McTaggart took her to a small Maine shipyard. Greenpeace volunteers spent almost three months working to put her back in shape. One of them was Peter Willcox, who had captained the Hudson River sloop *Clearwater* for four years, educating New Yorkers about the ecological plight of the polluted river. McTaggart made him captain of the repaired *Rainbow Warrior*.

With Willcox at the *Warrior*'s helm and McTaggart directing the efforts of Greenpeace International, a stunning number of victories for the environment were achieved. Combining direct action with behind-the-scenes pressure, they managed to shut down a New Jersey lead company that was dumping a million gallons of sulfuric acid into the ocean every day. While the *Warrior* crew blocked the hunt of seal pups, McTaggart's campaign induced Europe's Common Market to ban the commercial importation of baby seal skins. In McTaggart's campaign to save the whales, he combined direct action at sea against Japan, Peru, the U.S.S.R., Spain, Iceland, and Chile with confrontations on land. This led to the international Whaling Commission's July 1982 adoption of a world moratorium on whale hunting, except by natives for their food supply. But one year later McTaggart reported that two nations—the Soviet Union and Peru—were violating the moratorium. He sent the *Rainbow Warrior* to Siberian waters to photograph an illegal whaling operation.

Its crewmen went ashore near a whaling station to pass out anti-whaling leaflets to Soviet workers. They were arrested by soldiers at gunpoint. When the *Warrior* fled to escape seizure, it was pursued by a Soviet warship but managed to get away. "Seven people were arrested and put in prison," McTaggart reported. "That's the problem with the Russians. But we launched the operation on the day of the international meeting about whales. All the delegates saw the pictures of what was going on in Siberia."

Caught red-handed, the Soviets had to agree to shut down their whaling station. A protest from Washington also forced release of the Greenpeace prisoners after five days. Following the same strategy, Greenpeace compelled Peru to end its illegal whaling six months later.

In 1982 and 1983 McTaggart sent the *Rainbow Warrior* after tuna fleets in the South Pacific. They tried to get the fleets to stop using huge driftnets, which entangled and drowned thousands of dolphins. When the fleets refused, McTaggart started a consumer campaign to boycott all imported canned tuna that had been caught along with dolphin schools. A TV film of dolphins dying in the nets, shot by *Warrior* crews, won public support for the boycott. Soon United States canning companies began refusing to accept tuna caught without the safeguards for dolphins demanded by Greenpeace.

Greenpeace swimmers and inflatable blocking the path of
Nisshin Maru No. 3, *Tasman Sea.*
(© Greenpeace/Baker, 1990)

McTaggart also sent the *Warrior* into action against the dumping of big drums of nuclear waste by Britain, Switzerland, Belgium, and the Netherlands. The Zodiac crews who ran alongside the ships to block the dumping often risked life and limb when these confrontations turned ugly. But their courage helped bring about a London Dumping Convention that voted to make all dumping of nuclear wastes at sea illegal.

Greenpeace activists also took daredevil risks in perilous climbs to protest damage to the ecology. To dramatize the need to stop acid rain, they climbed huge smokestacks in Czechoslovakia, Western Europe, Canada, and the United States and set up protest banners. In 1984 they even scaled the Statue of

Liberty and hung a banner that read: GIVE ME LIBERTY FROM NUCLEAR WEAPONS. STOP TESTING.

By 1984 Greenpeace chapters had been established in fifteen countries, with half a million members in the United States alone. Its $10 million annual budget came from individual contributions averaging $10 apiece; from equipment donated by supportive companies; and from sales of Greenpeace merchandise. Part of their funds went to maintain the Greenpeace action fleet, which now consisted of four vessels.

From the very beginning of Greenpeace, McTaggart was convinced that his activists could win favor with, and support from, the public only by never resorting to violence, not even to protect themselves from violent opponents. He emphasized the importance of careful research into each of their projects, so that they could win TV debates with opponents and convince the public in TV, newspaper, and magazine interviews that they knew what they were talking about.

McTaggart also knew that humor could win public support and headlines. When United States Secretary of the Interior James Watts opened U.S. coasts to oil and gas drilling, McTaggart wanted to show that Watts had "lost his marbles." So he sent Greenpeacers to spill five thousand marbles onto Watts's office floor—a surefire headline winner.

McTaggart pronounced 1985 "the year of the Pacific" in order to focus world attention on United States nuclear tests in the Marshall Islands, on Japanese plans to dump nuclear wastes in the Pacific, and on the continuing French underground nuclear weapons testing in and around Mururoa atoll.

The people of Rongelap, one of the Marshall Islands, accused the U.S. Atomic Energy Commission (AEC) of having used them as nuclear guinea pigs. In 1954 a U.S. test of a fifteen-megaton hydrogen bomb, over one thousand times as powerful as the bomb dropped on Hiroshima, had exposed

105 Rongelap islanders to half a lethal dose of radiation. This had resulted, they charged, in a high death rate from leukemia, many birth defects, thyroid tumors, and other disorders.

The Rongelapese demanded to be moved to a radiation-free island. The United States and Marshall Island governments ignored them. Fearful of living any longer on their contaminated island, the Rongelapese appealed to Greenpeace to evacuate their 306 inhabitants to Mejato, an island out of the testing zone. McTaggart responded promptly by dispatching the *Rainbow Warrior* on what should have been the first of its several missions in "the Year of the Pacific."

When Peter Willcox sailed the *Warrior* into Rongelap, he was shocked by the effects of the hydrogen bomb's fallout on the inhabitants. "I can live with a lot of other problems," Willcox sighed, "but I was never able to be blasé about the deformed babies I saw in the Marshalls."

Greenpeace photographer Fernando Pereira recorded the evacuation of the Rongelapese and their belongings to their new home 120 miles away. To Washington's displeasure, his pictures and news of the event made front pages in the world press.

Meanwhile the presence of the *Warrior* in the Pacific did not go unnoticed by the French, who were planning new nuclear bomb tests—including a test of the devastating neutron bomb—at and around Mururoa atoll.

· TEN ·

INFORMATION THAT THE *WARRIOR* and four other Greenpeace vessels were planning to stop France's planned nuclear bomb tests was supplied by the French intelligence agency to French Defense Minister Charles Hernu. He conferred hastily with French Admiral Henry Fages to plot a strategy to thwart McTaggart. They were determined not to let Greenpeace cost them time, money, and manpower by tying up the tests, and not to let them embarrass France internationally.

Early in 1985 a young Frenchwoman who identified herself as Frédérique Bonlieu, an archaeologist and environmentalist, called at the New Zealand office of Greenpeace. She applied and was accepted as a volunteer worker.

On June 22 a yacht called the *Ouvéa*, manned by three "diving enthusiasts," arrived at New Zealand's Parengarenga Harbor from French New Caledonia. They were joined by Dr. Xavier Maniguet, a "specialist in diving medicine." The same day "Swiss newlyweds" Alain and Sophia Turenge flew into Auckland airport.

Soon afterward a Frenchman calling himself Jean Louis Dormand also flew in. He, it was later proved, was actually French Lieutenant-Colonel Louis-Pierre Dillais, who commanded a French naval base for frogmen. Bonlieu, the French divers, and the Turenges were all part of a DGSE secret mission headed by Dillais.

When Willcox and crew sailed the *Warrior* into Auckland harbor on July 7, they got an enthusiastic reception from the crowd greeting them. One of those who came aboard to welcome them was the new volunteer Bonlieu, who fraternized with the crew. When she persisted in asking questions about the *Warrior*'s plans, a crewman became suspicious and reported her actions to the New Zealand police.

Investigating Bonlieu, Auckland detectives ascertained that she was actually a French secret agent, Captain Christine Cabon. But by the time she was unmasked, she had already left the Greenpeace office and New Zealand. Her infiltration had provided the DGSE with a full dossier and timetable of McTaggart's plans to disrupt the neutron bomb tests.

On the evening of July 10, two frogmen in scuba gear dove beneath the *Rainbow Warrior* and planted two limpet bombs below the waterline on the ship's hull. When the frogmen surfaced nearby, they entered a waiting van driven by the Turenges. They were observed by suspicious boating club members, who wrote down the van's license plate.

All but a handful of the *Warrior*'s crew were ashore celebrating crewman Steve Sawyer's birthday. Captain Willcox was asleep below when the first bomb went off just before midnight. Jolted awake, he rushed to the engine room and found the *Warrior* taking on water rapidly. Water swelled upward toward deck level. Suddenly the second bomb exploded under the propeller.

The *Warrior* started to sink.

"Abandon ship!" Willcox yelled. He waited until he thought the last crewman aboard had scrambled to the dock before jumping himself. Looking around, he now realized that photographer Fernando Pereira was missing. But it was too late.

Next morning police divers recovered Pereira's body from the partially sunk *Warrior*. From his position, it was assumed he had rushed below to grab his camera after the first blast; the second blast had trapped and drowned him there.

McTaggart, who was in Britain lobbying the International Whaling Commission conference, was phoned immediately. "When our boat was sunk," he said later, "it was amazing. So many people said it was the French government, but I said it couldn't be . . . they couldn't be that stupid."

But McTaggart turned to his international contacts, and within five days he had proof that the order for sabotage had come from the highest levels of the French government. The French Ambassador to New Zealand completely denied France's involvement. But investigations by New Zealand detectives and French journalists soon verified McTaggart's findings.

A grim McTaggart held an international phone conference with his four other world directors. They all agreed that despite the loss of the *Warrior,* the other four small boats in the Greenpeace flotilla should sail for Mururoa as planned.

Some New Zealanders considered the attack on the *Warrior* a deliberate attack on New Zealand itself for identifying with Greenpeace's campaign for a nuclear-free Pacific. New Zealand police began the biggest manhunt in their history, involving one hundred detectives, to track down all the culprits involved in the sinking of the *Warrior* and the murder of Fernando Pereira.

· ELEVEN ·

NEW ZEALAND POLICE FOUND AN abandoned French Zodiac in Hobson Bay. Navy divers recovered two air tanks with French military markings in the harbor. When the Turenges returned a rented van, it was found to be the one reported as driving away the French scuba divers. On July 24 the Turenges were arrested and charged with being accessories in the bombing and murder of Pereira.

They were identified as French Intelligence agents Alain Mafart and Dominique Prieur. Mafart was allowed to call Paris. Police traced the number he called to the DGSE.

"I knew that the sabotage of the *Rainbow Warrior* had been ordered at the highest levels of the French government," McTaggart told me. "I had lived and worked in Paris for many years on my lawsuit against the French government. I had many friends in high and low places who had some very good access to information. I cannot really say more than that."

When Mitterand learned that four French magazines were preparing to publish stories flatly accusing the DGSE of sinking the *Warrior,* he quickly promised Prime Minister Lange "full cooperation" with inquiries by New Zealand police. And he appointed a high-ranking civil servant, Bernard Tricot, to investigate the affair and issue an "independent report."

McTaggart sped to France to seek a meeting with Mitterand, to confront him with the "real issue"—France's persistent nuclear tests in the South Pacific. The Prime Minister refused to see him. But McTaggart kept the *Rainbow Warrior* story alive by giving as many as twenty interviews a day to international journalists.

When Bernard Tricot issued his report, it conceded that the key actors in the affair were indeed French agents, but insisted that no evidence could be found linking them to the sinking of the *Warrior.* "My conclusion," he declared, "is that at no level could I say that anyone was guilty. . . . At the government level, no decision was taken aimed at damaging the *Rainbow Warrior.*" All the agents did, Tricot maintained, was simply spy on the Greenpeace crew.

"The report is too transparent to merit the description of whitewash!" snapped New Zealand Prime Minister Lange. Declaring that he had solid evidence linking the French with the sinking, he demanded an immediate apology by France for the "outrageous violation of our sovereignty."

Most of the French press also scoffed at the Tricot report as a government cover-up. Furious at Greenpeace, Mitterand warned McTaggart that if his protest flotilla left New Zealand for Mururoa, the French military would repel—"with force if necessary"—any ships that came within the "forbidden zone" of the atoll.

McTaggart refused to be intimidated. He dispatched a new flagship, donated by the Association of Maryland Pilots and christened the *Greenpeace IV,* to join the *Vega* and two other Greenpeace vessels nearing Mururoa. Mindful of the safety of the crews, he ordered all the ships to operate outside the twelve-mile limit imposed by France.

When French newspaper exposés of the *Warrior* sinking scandal began appearing, completely discrediting the Tricot report, French Prime Minister Laurius Fabius was forced to promise a new investigation. Then on September 22 he finally admitted that the *Warrior* had been sunk on direct orders from the DGSE. Defense Minister Charles Hernu was compelled to resign, and Admiral Pierre Lacoste was fired.

· TWELVE ·

MCTAGGART FLEW TO NEW ZEALAND for the trial of Mafart and Prieur on November 4. Through interviews with 150 international journalists covering the trial, McTaggart sought to pressure the French to compensate both the Pereira family and Greenpeace for their criminal act. By keeping the trial in world headlines, he also hoped to force the French government to restore its reputation by abandoning nuclear testing in the Pacific atolls.

McTaggart was angered when the court allowed the two French spies to plead guilty to a reduced charge of manslaughter, since they had not placed the bombs themselves. Mitterand asked that they be allowed to serve in France any sentence imposed. But New Zealand's chief justice sentenced both Mafart and Prieur to ten years in a New Zealand prison. Their crime, he declared, was a deliberate terrorist action, carried out for political motives, the first offense of its kind in New Zealand.

"People who come to this country and commit terrorist activities," he said, "cannot expect to have a short holiday at the expense of our Government and return home as heroes."

On July 7, 1986, a humiliated France was forced to pay

New Zealand $7 million in compensation for the sabotage. "The settlement," McTaggart told me, "was the result of an arbitration court's decision. It was made by a panel of judges—one French, one from New Zealand, and one Swiss." The French government also offered New Zealand an official apology.

New Zealand then allowed the transfer of Mafart and Prieur to a French military garrison for three more years in prison.

Greenpeace was awarded $8.16 million in damages.

The disabled *Rainbow Warrior* was towed out to sea and given a "fitting burial," becoming an underwater memorial to Greenpeace's valiant struggle to end nuclear explosions in the South Pacific.

Telegrams from around the world and donations amounting to $200,000 poured into New Zealand's Greenpeace offices. The money was used to establish a trust fund for Pereira's two children, and to replace the sunken ship. The sinking of the *Warrior* also brought Greenpeace 400,000 outraged new members.

No crusade McTaggart had dreamed up had ever brought such worldwide attention to a Greenpeace cause. And never before had he been able to stun a major government the way the *Warrior* scandal had rocked France. In essence, the French government in their violent overreaction to Greenpeace's nonviolent protest had played into McTaggart's hands.

Yet McTaggart was still unable to prevent the French from completing their nuclear tests in 1985. "As long as France continues testing nuclear weapons in the Pacific," McTaggart wrote Mitterand after the tests, "we will continue our peaceful protests."

Thirteen South Pacific nations signed a treaty banning the testing and placement of nuclear weapons and the dumping of

radioactive wastes in the South Pacific. And one of these nations was New Zealand, which branded the French tests "de-
plorable."

· THIRTEEN ·

IN DECEMBER 1986, MCTAGGART announced a new Greenpeace
target. Stating that the Mediterranean was "dying because of
chemical pollution," he declared, "We are now ready to open
offices in Italy and Spain for our 'Save the Mediterranean'
campaign."

By the end of 1986 Greenpeace had a contributing membership of over 1,500,000, with a budget of $11 million. Its
revenues grew larger and faster than those of any other environmental group, including the Sierra Club and National
Audubon Society. Its work was honored internationally when
Greenpeace was nominated in 1986 for the Nobel Peace Prize.

Although McTaggart's crusade to save the environment was
deadly serious, he could relax and laugh when some Greenpeacers encountered comic developments. Such was the case
when four activists trying to delay a U.S. nuclear test in the
Nevada desert became lost trying to find the Nevada test site.

Their jeep was halted by test site guards who demanded to
know what they were doing there. One Greenpeacer explained
that they were searching for wild ponies.

"Well," replied a guard, "don't go in *that* direction." He
pointed. "That's the Nevada test site."

The Greenpeacers thanked him profusely. Driving away in
a circular route, they managed to get to the test site in time to
delay the scheduled test.

The next year, McTaggart saw his concern about the effects of underwater atomic blasts on Mururoa validated.

Greenpeace scientists had speculated that if France exploded their new neutron bomb beneath the atoll, the island might sink into the sea, drowning its three thousand inhabitants, who had returned. When Jacques Cousteau, the famous oceanographer, visited the island, his divers ascertained that the atoll was deteriorating as a result of severe cracking and underwater slides caused by the tests.

In 1990 a new Greenpeace schooner, captained by Peter Willcox and rechristened *Rainbow Warrior,* took a two-month voyage through fogbound fishing grounds in the North Pacific. McTaggart's objective was to gather data and document the destruction of sea life, seabirds, and dolphins that were entangled and died in the driftnets used by more than six hundred Japanese, Taiwanese, and South Korean fishing fleets.

The new *Warrior,* with a crew of thirty from eleven different countries, conducted nonviolent protests against the vessels, launching its Zodiacs with divers and photographers. Sometimes they, too, became entangled in the driftnets, forcing the fishing vessels to stop and cut the Zodiacs loose.

Greenpeace's film documentation and testimony led to a UN resolution banning driftnetting. A law passed by Congress required the U.S. government to ban importation of any fish caught in driftnets once this resolution took effect.

In December 1990 the new *Rainbow Warrior* returned to Mururoa. Skirting the twelve-mile limit around the atoll, Greenpeacers collected samples that proved the seas there were radioactive. French authorities on the atoll refused the request of Greenpeace scientists to discuss this finding.

So the *Warrior* sent Zodiacs into the lagoon itself to test the extent of radioactivity there. These Greenpeacers were promptly arrested by forty French commandos and held for three hours before being released. When a second Greenpeace team entered the lagoon, they were seized, taken

ashore, and held incommunicado for three days. They were finally released when Greenpeacers around the world demonstrated in front of French consulates in six major cities.

In December 1990 McTaggart retired as chairman of
Greenpeace International. "I am now the honorary chairman
of the organization," he told me, "a position from which I can
help out in the political arena and provide what experience I
can. . . . I moved to Italy because I saw the Mediterranean is
where East meets West and South meets North. The area is rife
with political and religious and cultural tension. And yet the
protection of this sea is the one issue which unites people
across all those borders."

On April 8, 1992, it seemed as though McTaggart's long
struggle against France's nuclear tests in the South Pacific was
finally crowned with success. The French government declared that it would suspend all nuclear weapons testing, and
now urged other nations to follow their example.

But in November 1995, the French government suddenly
reversed itself and set off a series of six nuclear explosions—
with bombs three times as powerful as the one that destroyed
Hiroshima in 1945—beneath the Mururoa atoll. The French
also seized three Greenpeace protest ships at the site.

In France, Greenpeace activists deposited 2½ tons of
protest petitions with seven million signatures from all over
the world. Greenpeace demonstrators besieged French em-
bassies around the globe. Australian Prime Minister Paul
Keating termed the tests "an act of stupidity." At the United
Nations, ninety-five nations voted to condemn France's nuclear testing. To appease world anger, France vowed to do no
more testing after the sixth test and signed a treaty to that effect with the United States and England.

Members of McTaggart's Greenpeace continue to put themselves at physical and legal risk to protect sea creatures and

the environment. Greenpeace boats surround whaling ships and toxic waste dumping barges. Members interpose their bodies between seal packs and hunters' weapons. They hang from bridges to protest nuclear warships attempting to enter harbors.

Twenty-six years old in 1997, Greenpeace International had gathered 2.9 million dues-paying members, with a $145 million budget, one thousand full-time staff members, thirty-two offices worldwide and a fleet of oceangoing vessels. McTaggart stages at least ten ecological protests a month. His lobbying and public education campaigns persistently supplement Greenpeace action programs at sea and on land.

I asked McTaggart about the most important Greenpeace campaign he was involved in recently. "The biggest challenge I have been working on over the last few years," he replied, "is trying to get people to pay attention to what is going on in the former Soviet Union, and to get in there to help their critical environmental problems now. Russia and the other former Soviet republics are going to have to tear down an antiquated industrial base over the next decade, and replace it with something. For the sake of the entire planet, we need to make sure that the new industries which grow up there are clean and energy efficient."

I asked him if he was optimistic or pessimistic about the future of the ecology. "I'm afraid that I will remain pessimistic until I see a real change," he told me. "And real change is going to take some real commitment from places that now are only making noises about environmental protection—multinational corporations and the United States government, to name two."

The world owes an undying debt of gratitude to courageous David McTaggart and his fellow Greenpeace activists. They keep on fighting tirelessly to prevent the pollution of the earth's atmosphere, seas and water, and to protect our fellow creatures in the oceans. Thanks to them and those who join them, we and the generations that follow us will have a fighting chance to live on an earth made safe and kept beautiful for us all.

*Dave Foreman chained to the door of the visitors' center
in Grant Village, Yellowstone National Park, July 1986.*
(Photo courtesy Dave Foreman)

Dave Foreman

of Earth First!

1 9 4 6 –

"The Time for Talk Was Past"

SLEEPING BESIDE HIS WIFE, Dave Foreman was suddenly awakened when four men burst into his Tucson home on May 31, 1989.

"When I opened my eyes," he said, "I saw three guys standing around my bed pointing .357 Magnums at me. The first thing I thought of was Allen Funt and *Candid Camera.* Then they told me I was under arrest."

The three FBI agents dragged Foreman off to jail in his underpants. He was charged with having financed Earth First! activists who had been arrested for trying to cut the power line to a pumping plant along the Central Arizona Project. This was a controversial irrigation canal opposed by conservationists. The FBI claimed that the sabotage was a practice run for the planned disabling of three Western nuclear facilities.

Foreman faced a five-year prison sentence. "It was a shock," he declared, "but in the back of my mind I wasn't really surprised. The FBI never got the message that I retired from a leadership role in Earth First! a year ago. They wanted to make an example of me."

Earth First!, like Greenpeace, specialized in direct action to save the environment. Its members came out of the ranks of mainstream conservation groups, such as the Wilderness Society, the Sierra Club, and Friends of the Earth. They were activists who had grown impatient with compromise and were willing to use any nonviolent means to protect what remained of the American wilderness.

The chief activist and co-founder of Earth First! was rugged, bearded Dave Foreman, whose love of the outdoors had begun as a child. Born October 18, 1946, in Albuquerque, New Mexico, he moved constantly with his family as his father, an Air Force sergeant, was assigned to new posts. He spent his early years in the Philippines, where he grew to love the island's rainforests, which his family visited on frequent excursions.

During his family's many moves, the one thing that remained constant in Dave's life was his joy in exploring the forests near each new home. His love of the outdoors, fostered by his conservation-minded parents, led him to the Boy Scouts, where he achieved Eagle rank. In high school he was an enthusiastic backpacker and rapids rafter, activities which deepened his appreciation of the beauty of the unspoiled wilderness.

In the anti-establishment sixties, Dave was a political conservative as well as a conservationist. When he entered the University of New Mexico, he joined the conservative Young Americans for Freedom. After graduating in 1968, full of gung-ho patriotism, he signed up with the Marines, anticipating a vigorous, fulfilling life in the outdoors. In officers' candidate school, however, he grew incensed by the humiliation candidates were forced to endure in order to break their sense of individuality and compel blind obedience to orders.

"On the second day," Foreman told me, "my worlds collided and I realized their inconsistency. . . . By 1968 I was also beginning to have some doubts about the war in Vietnam, and beginning to question some of my assumptions about conservatism. I was in the Marine Corps sixty-one days—and thirty-one days were spent in the brig for defying officers and going AWOL. Enlisting in the Marine Corps was the worst mistake I ever made, but it was a learning experience."

He left the Marine Corps with an "undesirable" discharge.

Confused over the loss of his values, Foreman suffered something of a nervous breakdown. For a while he worked at a cousin's trading post on an Indian reservation, attended a horseshoeing school, and resumed backpacking and river rafting.

His love of the outdoors made him want to conserve the wilderness which contributed so much to his enjoyment of life. "I began to be disturbed," he told me, "by dam proposals in New Mexico, and by more roads and logging operations in the wilderness. So by 1971 I started writing letters of protest and contacting various conservationists. I met folks in Santa Fe who had started several environmental groups. In the spring of 1972 I returned to the University of New Mexico to go to graduate school in biology.

"After the Marine Corps I was pretty burned out about politics, but at the university I gave a couple of speeches against the Vietnam War and against CIA recruiting on campus. Those caused a bit of a stir since I'd been the university chairman for the [conservative] Young Americans for Freedom.

"Then for eighteen months I worked on the U.S. Forest Service's RARE-1 program, the first Roadless Area Review and Evaluation, to identify the last roadless areas in the national forests. That led to a job with the Wilderness Society."

After a training session with the society in 1973, Foreman became the Arizona/New Mexico regional representative. Organizing a conservation campaign for the area's environmentalists, he formed a strong bond with idealistic young men like himself dedicated to saving the earth.

"We realized that we would not receive the salary we could earn in government or private industry but we didn't expect it," Foreman explained. "We were working for nonprofit groups funded by the contributions of concerned people. . . . We didn't want to get rich."

He ran a little business on the side as a mule packer in the Gila wilderness. "Before leaving for Washington, D.C., to tes-

tify at hearings," he said, chuckling, "I'd walk around the cor-
ral in my cowboy boots, so when I'd enter the hearing room in
Congress, I'd have manure on my boots, looking like a real
cowboy. The congressmen were surprised, saying, 'Gosh,
there's a guy who actually runs mules for the wilderness.' It
wrecked their preconception that all environmentalists were
yuppy suburbanites."

· T W O ·

IN 1977 FOREMAN WAS SENT to the Washington office as a full-
time lobbyist for the Wilderness Society. He had to give up the
working cowboy image, for in Washington he had to appear to
be a moderate, to convince congressmen that they could both
preserve the wilderness and support the production of meat,
timber, or minerals, and that clean air and water actually
benefited the economy.

Foreman was shocked at how many administration officials and congressmen posed as supporters of environmental
bills, only to cripple such legislation with restrictions demanded by mining, timber, and livestock industries—industries that made large contributions to election campaign
funds.

From 1977 to 1979 Foreman worked coordinating the efforts of conservation groups around the country to pressure the
United States Forest Service into keeping 66 million acres of
unroaded wilderness under federal protection. But the Forest
Service knuckled under to the timber, mining, and grazing industries, and gave them access to 51 million acres.

"They tried to justify the cutback," Foreman told me, "by
claiming the need for timber cutting and forestry jobs. Worse,
the 15 million acres we won were basically scenic, high ele-
vation country okay for backpackers, but not important for

preserving the wildlife habitat. They were just throwing us a bone.

"We didn't ask for much. We were very reasonable. And we lost. By that time Congress and all the conservationist groups were being afraid of our own shadow. We felt we were causing a backlash by asking too much. The reality was that we were not asking for *enough*, only emboldening the traditional opponents of conservation, who distributed big money as election campaign contributions."

Foreman was disillusioned with the conservation movement, and disgusted with the Forest Service for betraying its public trust. He protested to the Assistant Secretary of Agriculture in charge of the Forest Service, only to get more excuses. He had originally been heartened by the 1976 election of avowed conservationist Jimmy Carter as president, and by Carter's appointment of Foreman's colleagues to key positions in his administration.

"We'd think, oh boy, they'll really be able to help us," Foreman recalled. "Then we'd go to a meeting, and they'd lobby us more than we'd lobby them. We'd hear, 'Look, the president's in trouble with this senator or these interests, so could you lay back, take a softer approach?' And we would."

He added ruefully, "We had lost to the timber, mining, and cattle interests on every point. . . . I thought, if this is how we're treated by our friends, something is seriously wrong with our strategy. We clearly needed a harder-nosed approach."

At about this time Foreman also grew disillusioned with the national leadership of the Wilderness Society. A new director hired in the fall of 1978 had little interest in continuing the staff's efforts to work with grass-roots groups. He wanted them instead to go out after big grants, to appear more professional and Washington-oriented, and to pursue credit and publicity for the Wilderness Society.

Foreman noticed this trend in other large environmental groups—Sierra Club, Friends of the Earth, and the Audubon Society—as well. Local members and field staffs were often deterred from direct challenges that could upset the national organizations' policy of "reasonable moderation."

Foreman grew more and more skeptical about pinning the hopes of environmentalists on lobbying in Washington. "Environmentalists were more concerned with lining up a future job with some powerful senator or congressman," he said, "than with the battles that needed to be fought. . . . We got beat badly. The time for talk was past."

· **THREE** ·

THE LAST STRAW FOR FOREMAN occurred when the governing body of the Wilderness Society began to bring onto their council millionaires with a vague environmental interest, blurring the distinction between serious conservationists and big business interests. Nevertheless he didn't quit the Wilderness Society.

Despondent over the hopelessness of his struggle in Washington, and worn out from working eighty-hour weeks for eight years, Foreman was plunged into even deeper gloom by a divorce. For a while, like David McTaggart, he drowned his sorrows in alcohol. Finally, in January 1989 he obtained a six-month sabbatical leave. Throwing a sleeping bag into his old van, he sped out of Washington, heading back to Glenwood, New Mexico.

"Basically I just recuperated," Foreman told me. "I hiked a lot and sought to get my energy back. I saw an article in *The New York Times* on RARE-II, focusing on the Gila National Forest in New Mexico. They quoted a rancher I had considered a friend, and reasonable on conservation issues, saying I was lucky I was still alive; that a lot of the ranchers had thought about shooting me. A few days later I was walking to the post office, and greeted four 'good old boys' I knew. They didn't return my greeting. But after I passed one growled, 'There's the son-of-a-bitch we oughta kill!' I turned and asked them why they wanted to kill me. One said, 'That's because you're trying to lock up the whole national forest!'"

Foreman resumed his old job as the Wilderness Society's Southwest representative, but only after being assured he would essentially be left alone to work on saving 180 million acres of scenic Western public lands from overgrazing by ranchers. This area was managed by the Department of the Interior's Bureau of Land Management (BLM) which recognized that overgrazing was a serious problem. Tracts had been stripped of grass, allowing erosion to send millions of tons of topsoil into Western rivers. Wildlife habitat was wiped out, and wilderness areas faced ruin. So when Foreman agitated to save these public lands, the BLM agreed to cut back the number of animals grazing on them.

"But after the expected outcry from the few thousand ranchers leasing BLM land and their political cronies in Congress and state capitals," Foreman related, "BLM backtracked so quickly that a fair number of knees must have been dislocated. Why were BLM and the Department of the Interior so gutless?"

At about this time Foreman became intrigued by *The Monkey Wrench Gang*, a novel by Edward Abbey. It dealt with four renegade environmentalists who plot to cripple bulldozers, cut power lines, blow up an empty mining train, and demolish a highway bridge, and who dream of blowing up Glen Canyon Dam to end its flooding of the scenic canyon. Foreman wrote a review of the book for the *High Country News*.

"I wrote that many conservationists considered the Monkey Wrench Gang an embarrassment," he told me, "but they gave a lot of us vicarious pleasure. The book talked about things none of us would do, but which we enjoyed reading about. And it changed the image of conservationists, who were always regarded as effete urban wimps, to tough activists. That was important."

Restless waiting for more dynamic conservation action, Foreman phoned a conservationist friend, Howie Wolke, who was working as bouncer at a bar in Jackson, Wyoming. "Howie," he said, "I've left the Wilderness Society. I'm fed up with the environmental movement."

"I know what you mean," Wolke replied. "They're letting the S.O.B.'s drive roads into the wilderness all over, cutting trees and sinking wells, and wiping out the bears. Hey, let's take a camping trip and talk about doing something to stop it."

Wolke's old van collected other mutual friends: Mike Roselle, who had organized Construction Workers for Wilderness; Bart Koehler, Wyoming representative for the Wilderness Society; and conservationist Ron Kezar. They drove to New Mexico to pick up Foreman, then headed south into Mexico's Pinaeate Desert.

Over campfires and beers in a bar in San Luis Sonora, the five friends discussed Abbey's novel and came to a decision.

"We said, 'Okay, it's time to quit talking,'" Foreman told me. "'Let's start something.' I came up with the name Earth First! We all agreed we needed a tougher conservation group."

Such a group might help make mainstream environmental programs look moderate by comparison, increasing their chances of making the Establishment more willing to deal with them. "That was really one of our objectives," Foreman told me.

· FOUR ·

WHEN THEY RETURNED FROM Mexico, Foreman and Wolke set Earth First! in motion. "We set out to be radical in style, positions, philosophy, and organization in order to be effective," Foreman told me, "and to avoid the pitfalls of cooption and moderation we had already experienced."

He pointed out that the name Earth First! emphasized that the well-being of the earth and all its life forms came before any other considerations, a reflection of the philosophies of John Muir and Rachel Carson. "All living beings have the same right to be here," Foreman asserted. Everything on earth was connected; humans and their goals were not the ultimate or sole reason for life on the planet.

Foreman and Wolke formulated a long-range goal of withdrawing huge areas and turning them into wilderness sanctuaries. Their aims included reclaiming ploughed lands, freeing rivers by tearing down dams that blocked them, protecting wilderness creatures by leaving their habitat unviolated, and saving centuries-old giant trees from the chain saws of loggers.

Foreman and the other Earth First!ers determined to keep their activities confrontational but within the law, and to inspire others to follow their radical example. They sought to win results where moderate environmentalism had failed, through the publicity that throwing "a monkey wrench in the work of progress" would bring.

At first Foreman's monkeywrenchers initiated actions that were largely symbolic and theatrical, seeking photo opportunities rather than inflicting damage. Earth First! tactics, Foreman explained, included "politics in the streets, civil disobedience, media stunts, and holding the enemies of conservation up to ridicule," to expose industrial exploitation.

On March 21, 1981, Earth First! held its first national

gathering at Glen Canyon Dam in Arizona. Seventy-five members lined the Colorado River Bridge with signs reading "Damn Watt [Reagan's Secretary of the Interior], not Rivers" and "Free the Colorado." Some Sierra Club members attended unofficially.

Edward Abbey, author of *The Monkey Wrench Gang*, spoke to the gathering, demanding abolition of the dam. Evoking memories of the "green and living wilderness" that had been Glen Canyon nineteen years earlier, he cried, "And they took it away from us. The politicians of Arizona, Utah, New Mexico, and Colorado, in cahoots with the land developers, city developers, industrial developers of the Southwest, stole this treasure from us in order to pursue and promote their crackpot ideology of growth, profit, and power. . . . And if opposition is not enough, we must resist. And if resistance is not enough, then subvert!"

Foreman was very much impressed with Abbey. "He had a reputation larger than life," he said, "but he was a very down-to-earth, open, friendly person. He was the best listener I've ever known."

At the rally's culmination, Foreman, Wolke, and three others perched on top of the dam. Shouting, "Earth First!" they unfurled a twenty-one-foot-wide black plastic cloth down the face of the dam. It created the terrifying effect of a growing three-hundred-foot crack.

Even though Earth First! hadn't contacted the media, the stunt got a tremendous amount of news coverage. It set the tone for further Earth First! demonstrations, and brought more than a thousand new applications for membership from all over the United States. It also attracted the attention of the FBI, which dusted the Glen Canyon Dam for fingerprints of the perpetrators.

The successful stunt was repeated at the Elwha Dam in

Earth First! "cracks" Glen Canyon Dam, March 21, 1981.
(Photo courtesy Dave Foreman)

Washington, and also at the Hetch Hetchy Dam in California—the area John Muir had tried so hard to save—where they posted a sign reading, FREE THE RIVERS!

Foreman liked to use a light touch in the stunts planned by Earth First! "There was a real feeling of being the clown prince of the environmental movement," he said, smiling. "We were comic relief." As one of their stunts to save the desert from being torn up in 1983 by off-road motorcycles, the monkeywrenchers rearranged the course markers of a desert race. A hundred puzzled motorcyclists plunged into a blind ravine.

The Earth First!ers toured college and rural towns around the West with their message that people should have no higher status on earth than bears, wolves, rivers, or trees. They asked that all employees of conservation groups be given a two-week paid vacation every year in the wilderness. And they demanded a "Wilderness Preservation System" that would protect no less than 716 million acres, and offered solid research to justify the plan.

In July 1982 some four hundred monkeywrenchers showed up for Earth First!'s third annual Round River Rendezvous to protest the planned drilling of an oil well in a roadless area.

When a New Mexico oil company built an illegal road through the wilderness in October, Foreman, Wolke, and other Earth First!ers blocked the company's vehicles from using the road. In retaliation, the company bulldozed their camp flat. Unfortunately for the company, CBS Evening News was on hand to record its criminal act. National news coverage transformed Earth First! into a serious national movement.

· FIVE ·

JUBILANT, DAVE FOREMAN TURNED up the heat. In 1983, when Reagan's anti-conservation Secretary of the Interior, James

Watt, addressed a Western Governors' Conference at Jackson, Wyoming, he received an unpleasant surprise.

"We had three hundred people show up to stage what was probably the noisiest, most energetic anti-Watt demonstration ever held," Foreman said with a grin. "A bunch of loggers who had come to Jackson to make trouble for us looked around and noticed that we had them considerably outnumbered, and quietly . . . headed home. . . . The upshot of it all was that the environmental causes we were there to champion got the lion's share of media attention, while Watt and his supporters got nothing but red faces."

Foreman and his colleagues organized roving SWAAT (Save Wilderness At Any Time) teams. These activists, drawn from all over the West, sabotaged bulldozers and stood in front of machines to blockade logging roads and stop the denuding of forests.

Protesting Watt's pro-business policies, they also occupied Forest Service offices in Oregon, Texas, Washington, and Wyoming. When attempts were made to dislodge them, they fought to remain, and were arrested and jailed.

In May 1983 the Forest Service began building a logging access road through the Kalmiopsis Wilderness of Oregon. Local environmentalists appealed to Foreman and Earth First! for help. Together they decided to blockade construction of the road.

"We expected severe opposition," Foreman recalled, "so everybody who was to be involved with the action underwent several hours of nonviolent tactics training in order to be prepared. In all, we staged seven blockades over a two-month period."

When Foreman refused to get out of the way of a logger's truck, the driver kept going, pushing Foreman the length of a football field. "I hold the world's record for the truck-assisted backwards hundred-yard dash," Foreman said, smiling. "I finally fell and held on to the bumper while I was being dragged by the truck. It eventually stopped when they got worried they might have killed me. A deputy sheriff right behind them came up and asked if I was severely injured. When I said I didn't think so, he said, 'Well, good, you're under arrest.' And he hauled me off as the driver of the truck jumped out and yelled at me, 'You rotten Communist bastard, why don't you go back where you came from!' I knew the man, so I replied, 'But, Les, I'm a registered Republican.' That *really* infuriated him."

Foreman's knees were pretty banged up, but he was otherwise unhurt. He and forty-four other Earth First!ers spent five hours in jail before they were bailed out. In the early days of Earth First! bail and fines were fairly small. People paid their own fines, or local activists raised the money for them.

"We got a great deal of media attention," Foreman said. "Our blockades bought time and slowed construction of the road, so that the Oregon Natural Resources Council and Earth First! were able to file a lawsuit. . . . The suit was a resounding success. . . . The road was stopped, and we had a preliminary injunction against its continuation. It was a major victory for Earth First! and for the thousands of Oregonians who—once they were made aware of what was happening in and to their state—wrote letters, made phone calls, and attended meetings to help get the road stopped."

President Reagan tried to reverse this victory by signing a bill removing the area affected from designation as an official wilderness. But significantly, the Forest Service decided not to risk trying to build the access road again.

"The Forest Service is shying away from another confrontation with us," Foreman observed. "It's conclusive evidence of the power of non-violent direct action."

By 1984 there were Earth First! chapters in most of the

fifty states. At that year's Earth First! rendezvous near Libby, Montana, Foreman told his activists, "It's time we stand up . . . and say to those who are destroying nature, 'No more! This is where we make our stand. And if you intend to cut down the last old-growth Douglas fir in Oregon, you'll have to cut *me* first! If you want to kill the last grizzly in the Cabinet Mountains, then you'd better use the first bullet on *me!* If you plan to dam the last wild river in California, you'll have to dump the first load of concrete on *me!*'"

· SIX ·

IN MID-1985, FOREMAN PRIVATELY published a ten-dollar manual called *Eco-defense: A Field Guide to Monkeywrenching,* and designated it "for entertainment purposes only." He added, tongue in cheek, "No one involved with this book . . . encourages anyone to do any of the stupid, illegal things contained herein." But he also wrote, "It is time to act heroically and admittedly illegally in defense of the wild."

The book described various methods of spiking trees, destroying billboards, disabling helicopters, removing signs from snowmobile trails and surveyors' roads, blocking wilderness road building, freeing animals from hunters' traps, downing power lines, and damaging earth-moving equipment—all while wearing camouflage and avoiding detection and arrest. It also insisted that an act in defense of the environment was really a form of civil disobedience—resistance to an unjust law.

Foreman considered monkeywrenching just one extremely moral way of resisting the state-supported industrialization of nature. Other ways included lobbying, writing letters, filing lawsuits. Officially, Earth First! did not encourage monkeywrenching, but instead left that decision up to individual activists.

The practice of monkeywrenching became known as ecotage, and its activists as ecoteurs. The more conservative environmental organizations, disturbed by Earth First!'s tactics, frowned on them as "saboteurs" and "radicals." One official said testily, "I see no difference between destroying a river and destroying a bulldozer."

"It's important to understand," Foreman insisted, "that monkeywrenching is *not* vandalism. . . . While monkeywrenching is undertaken with purpose and respect, and with the highest moral standards in mind, vandalism is senseless and hurtful."

The *real* vandals, he accused, were those who wanted to destroy America's last wildernesses. Earth First!'s tactics were based on a perception that government agencies and private industry were collaborating in the rape of public lands.

One of the more controversial tactics of Earth First! was stopping the lumbering of old-growth forests by driving nails into tree trunks. This made the trees useless as lumber, and damaged expensive mill buzzsaws.

"I had never heard of this," Foreman told me, "until it was explained to me by some loggers in Montana. Actually, the technique was first used by the Wobblies [Industrial Workers of the World, or IWW] in lumber strikes early in the century."

In 1984 some twelve thousand nails were driven into twenty-one thousand acres of British Columbia trees. Just before a timber harvest in Virginia in the spring of 1985, the forest superintendent received a letter that read: "Speaking on behalf of the trees, rocks and wildlife of the George Washington National Forest, this is to inform you that approximately 40 pounds of spikes have been inserted in the trees at various locations. . . . Good luck finding them. Good riddance to any saws that ever do find them. (Signed) Rednecks for Wilderness."

Tree spiking caused adverse publicity, however, when a mill buzzsaw hit a spike in a lumbered tree and a mill worker was seriously injured. Earth First! denied that its organization was involved. Foreman stated that their goal was to prevent logging, not harm any workers.

Earth First!ers increasingly felt they had to resort to more imaginative tactics to attract attention to their protests. To protest housing that had been built in Yellowstone's grizzly bear habitat, some of the seventy activists dressed in bear costumes and demanded salmon dinners from puzzled but amused tourists.

Foreman chained himself to the visitors' center. He and eighteen others were arrested and bused to jail. The bus paused en route at the sight of a mother grizzly strolling with two cubs. "It was a sign," Foreman said, "that we were doing the right thing." Some of the "bears" remained in costume during their arraignment by an amused Federal magistrate. One of them sang a song as his defense plea. The "bears" and the other Earth First!ers each received a fifty dollar or one hundred dollar fine.

· SEVEN ·

IN 1985 THE CHEVRON OIL COMPANY attempted to build a road through the Bridger-Teton National Forest in Wyoming to facilitate oil exploration. The orange-tipped stakes for the road placed by surveyors were twice pulled out, baffling the road-builders. In June, when stakes were driven in a third time, a Chevron employee caught Howie Wolke, who was now a wilderness guide, pulling up the stakes again. Wolke was held at hatchetpoint for arrest. Ordered to pay Chevron damages, he was sentenced to six months in jail, becoming the first Earth First!er to be jailed for monkeywrenching, or ecotage.

"The judge was waiting for a sign of remorse," Wolke recalled, "but I was pretty remorseless. The only thing I regret is that the papers say I took up a hundred yards of stakes. It was more like five miles!"

Prosecutors demanded that Wolke turn over Earth First!'s membership list. He replied truthfully that there was no such formal list. He explained later that none was kept partly to foil investigators "because we don't always stay within the bounds of the law." Foreman's reason was to avoid setting up a bureaucratic organization with officers, bylaws, and an expense-eating overhead.

Earth First! operated through a network of contacts across the country that rounded up members swiftly as needed for local operations. Members were a collection of men and women committed to supporting each other in preserving the wilderness.

Based on the subscriptions to his newsletter, Foreman estimated that by January 1985, Earth First! had enlisted some ten thousand American members, "with the number growing rapidly." Earth First!ers were also active in Australia and Japan. "Even the premier of the Western Solomon Islands is an Earth First!er," Foreman revealed proudly.

Working for Earth First! full time, and editing the activists' newsletter, Foreman was paid only expenses plus $250 a month "for survival necessities."

"So far as anybody having a big salary and a formal job, no thank you," Foreman said. "There will never be anybody working for Earth First! on a career basis, and pulling down $20,000 or $30,000 a year or more, as is the rule in many of the larger environmental groups. . . . Fat salaries like that are counterproductive—they attract the wrong sort of people to the environmental movement, and they waste members' contributions."

At that time, Foreman's wife was a cardiac care nurse, and it was her salary that essentially supported them.

While Mike Roselle went on the road organizing new Earth First! chapters, Foreman directed activities from his home in Tucson. He was soon compelled to cease monkey-wrenching himself because his presence tipped off Forest Service authorities that an Earth First! action was about to occur. He was easily recognized because he had been in the forefront of innumerable acts of civil disobedience, and had been arrested seven times.

"Obviously," he grinned wryly, "I'm a prime suspect."

In July 1985, environmentalists in Oregon learned that the Forest Service had turned over the Willamette National Forest to lumber interests. They appealed to Dave Foreman for help. He promptly dispatched Mike Roselle to work out preventive tactics. Soon ecoteurs fanned out through the forest spiking the trees. The Forest Service was kept busy for weeks using metal detectors and crowbars to locate and remove the nails.

Activists chained themselves to Douglas firs with bicycle locks. Demonstrations and blockades drew the press, which recorded more than one hundred arrests. Most dramatic was the Earth First!ers' takeover of the forest canopy. Men and women activists climbed half a dozen of the biggest trees in the Cathedral Forest and erected small plywood platforms eighty feet above the ground. They hauled up provisions to last twenty-seven days and hung banners reading, WILLAMETTE INDUSTRIES—OUT OF CATHEDRAL FOREST! Since they were too high to be reached by mechanical cherry pickers, they challenged the frustrated lumbermen to cut down the trees—an act that would mean death to the protest-

ers. When the company began cutting down trees around
them, NBC carried the story on the evening news. Local officials angrily ordered both the Forest Service and Willamette
Industries to stop their assault on the forest.

"I've seen heroism," Foreman observed, "people climbing
to the tops of eighty-foot trees to keep them from being cut
down, people lying under bulldozers, people going to jail. . . .
Ecotage is a way someone can empower himself."

Earth First!ers' "guerrilla theater" has proved effective
both in calling national attention to the rape of the environment and in winning support to stop it. In many cases they
were able to hamper or close down assaults on the wilderness.

Monkeywrenching, Foreman insisted, was not only morally
justified, but morally required. "When you look closely," he
said, "at the unholy assault the industrial state is mounting
against the public's wildlands . . . the full-scale, all-out war being waged against ecosystems all over the world—it forces you
to consider any and all means of resisting that destruction."

Earth First!, he pointed out, was also changing the image
of environmentalists: "It was ridiculous that off-roaders [off-
road vehicle riders] were macho men, and backpackers were
considered wimps. We're not accepting the rules of the game
any more!"

· EIGHT ·

THE MORE EFFECTIVE FOREMAN and Earth First! became in
fighting for the wilderness, the more bitterly they were
attacked by the Forest Service and big business. The mainstream environmental organizations were also critical, com-
plaining that they were upsetting the fragile legitimacy the
conservation movement had won over the previous two
decades.

Many moderate conservationists shared the view of Jay Hair, president of the National Wildlife Federation, who called the group "outlaws" and "terrorists [who] have no right being considered environmentalists." But others saw Foreman and his band as folk heroes who risked jail and their lives to right environmental wrongs. Many Earth First!ers even relished the view that they were ecological "outlaws," fighting oppression with the bravado spirit of Robin Hood's men in Sherwood Forest. They also identified with anti-Vietnam activists of the sixties, which some had been. Many drank beer, wore cowboy boots, and drove pickup trucks with bumper stickers reading, REDNECKS FOR WILDERNESS.

"Earth First! would be big enough," Foreman declared, "to contain street poets and cowboy bar bouncers, agnostics and pagans, vegetarians and raw steak eaters, pacifists and those who think turning the other cheek is a good way to get a sore face."

In 1986 as many as a thousand cars and trucks crowded into the little Idaho Valley where the seventh Round River Rendezvous was held, much to Foreman's dismay.

"Next summer we're not going to tell anybody where the Rendezvous is," he sighed. "Next summer, people will just have to know. We're getting too damn big."

Activists at the Rendezvous swapped stories about their monkeywrenching and jail time. One activist told Foreman he had done "felony time" in Oregon for sawing down a billboard, an act he termed a lot more environment-friendly than sawing down a tree. Foreman told him, "You made the same damn mistake Howie Wolke did. You got caught."

Campers at the Rendezvous had a bigger worry than arrest. Three dozen anti-environmentalist vigilantes were reported to be packing guns and preparing to attack the Rendezvous campsite. Foreman himself chased off one

*Dave Foreman arrested at Grand Canyon National Park
uranium mine demonstration, March 1987.*
(Photo courtesy Dave Foreman)

vigilante scout who broke into the campsite on a dirt bike. Just how real the threat of vigilante violence was would never be known, because county sheriffs and Forest Service personnel rushed up the canyon, allegedly to disperse the vigilantes.

Foreman, however, wasn't sure what to make of the "rescue." He had earlier been tipped off by Forest Service members friendly to his cause that the Forest Service had planted undercover agents in Earth First! as part of an ongoing infiltration program organized by the Federal Law Enforcement Training Center.

In 1988 Foreman shocked Earth First! members when he announced that he was stepping down as their leader. "I gave up editorship of the Earth First! journal in May," he told me. "I had been planning to do it for some time because I felt I needed more freedom to do what I wanted to do. I was talking with Tom Hayden, who had helped found Students for a Democratic Society in the sixties. We agreed that groups like that, Earth First!, the Black Panthers, or the Indian movement had an effective life really of only about seven years.

"After that you develop so much media baggage, so much problem with image, that you really aren't in control any more. Also, you develop a radical image and begin to attract a lot of people who don't understand what you're really for. Some counter-culture factions wanted Earth First! to attack the Establishment instead of remaining a conservation group, so I felt the organization had lost its essential purpose. I didn't think a battle to control Earth First! would be beneficial.

Foreman remained active in Earth First!, but spent much of his free time at home writing *Confessions of an Eco-Warrior*, a book about his struggles as a conservationist.

The year Foreman retired from Earth First!, a personable, quiet "redneck for wilderness" joined a group of Earth

First!ers in Tucson. He introduced himself as Mike Tait, an emotionally troubled Vietnam veteran eager to join in radical environmental action. He began dating Peg Millet of the Earth First! Speakers Bureau, and soon was invited to dine at Foreman's house. That summer he attended the annual Round River Rendezvous in Washington state, and began taking part in wilderness actions.

After Mike had become a fixture at Earth First! meetings and protests, he proposed a dangerous action to Mark Davis, a cabinetmaker, along with activists Peg Millet and Mark Baker: that they cut the power line of the pumping plant along the Central Arizona project. When they agreed, Tait urged Davis to get funding for the plan from Foreman.

In March 1989 Foreman did give Davis some money from an Earth First! yard sale, but only "to help on whatever work you want to do." When Tait began to talk enthusiastically about sabotaging nuclear plants, Foreman immediately objected.

"Just stop the plan!" he said sharply. "I am not a part of this. . . . You don't get support for your movement by frightening people."

But the four monkeywrenchers went off to carry out Tait's plan to cut power to the pumping plant along the Central Arizona Project. Because Davis didn't know how to use a propane cutting torch, another new member named Ron Frazier taught him and drove him to buy one. Frazier also encouraged Davis to buy army incendiary thermite grenades from a source Frazier found for him. Getting nervous, Davis told Tait he'd decided to give up monkeywrenching. But Tait talked him back into it.

On the night of May 30, 1989, the four activists entered the Arizona desert, and began trying to blowtorch the legs off a powerline tower. Suddenly the desert sky lit up with flares.

Some fifty heavily armed FBI agents equipped with night-vision goggles rushed to pounce upon the Earth First! activists.

· N I N E ·

PEG MILLET, MARK DAVIS, and Mark Baker were seized and taken into custody. Mike Tait mysteriously disappeared. Early next morning, the FBI broke into Dave Foreman's home and arrested him. It was only then that Foreman began to suspect Mike Tait was an FBI agent provocateur.

Gerry Spence, a Jackson, Wyoming, attorney, was outraged by Foreman's arrest. "It opens the door," he warned, "to the political persecution of people who raise their voices against mainstream America." He agreed to defend Foreman without charge.

Millet, Davis, and Baker were held in jail without bail as "a threat to the community." Foreman, released on bail after two days, accused the FBI of a blatant attempt to destroy Earth First! and deliver a warning to the environmental movement.

"The FBI thinks that it can knock me out," he declared, "since they think of me as the leader of Earth First! Then they can knock out the entire movement. But I'm not important to Earth First! in its day-to-day functioning."

After his arrest, Foreman warned Earth First!ers, "Monkeywrenching will have to be different. People are going to have to zip their lips—they'll have to become a lot more security-conscious. . . . It's one thing having fun tweaking the nose of the Establishment. It's something completely different when they come in with guns and thirty-five-year jail sentences."

The arrests of the five Earth First! activists shocked the organization, but during the two years between the arrests and the trial, they did not deter new members from joining. More distressing was the increasing willingness of anti-environmentalists to use violence to protect their interests.

In June 1989 Northern California timber company officials exchanged letters praising acts of violence against environmentalists by vigilantes. That feeling was echoed by many in the timber industry.

In August 1989 Earth First!ers blockaded an access road to three hundred forest acres that were being logged by Doyle Lancaster. When one activist banged a split log against a logger's truck, the driver tried to run down the demonstrators. Activist Judi Bari was involved in a brawl with the loggers. A few days later the same logging truck rear-ended Bari's car, sending her semi-conscious to the hospital. "I had an awful time deciding that I was to go on after that," she said. "I mean, is this worth the risk?"

Judi Bari continued to work with Earth First! She was one of the organizers of Redwood Summer, a ten-week event beginning in June 1990. Hundreds of activists from several different environmental groups all united to prevent logging in California's magnificent redwood forests.

On May 24, 1990, a pipe bomb blew up the car of Judi Bari and activist Darryl Cherney, crippling Bari for life. The two were accused of having made and transported the bomb themselves, and were subjected to "vigorous interrogation," although charges were never filed.

On the pretext of searching for the would-be assassin, law enforcement officials ransacked the homes of environmentalists throughout Northern California. To the delight of the California timber industry, they described the growing nonviolent Redwood Summer movement as "terrorist." The FBI was forced to drop its investigation of Bari and Cherney when it became clear that they were innocent victims.

In September 1990 Dave Foreman stunned Earth First!ers
once more by announcing that he was withdrawing totally from
the movement. He said the movement had been taken over
by those who identified "more with the Left than with the conservation movement," and who were "inspired more by the
writings of sixties' Yippee [counter-culture radical] Abby
Hoffman than those of Edward Abbey." He had not withdrawn
before, he explained, because he did not want to give the impression of doing so because of FBI charges against him.

It was understandable, Foreman said, to want to fight
against wilderness destruction. Under his leadership, Earth
First! had saved thousands of acres of virgin forest and
brought the issue to national attention. But the troubling question was how far to go in battling the destroyers.

"I don't believe," he declared, "that muddying the issues
with a lot of class-struggle rhetoric or weird lifestyle stuff
works. Generally you are most effective when you remain part
of society." He felt that the group's image as a bunch of aging
hippies had alienated mainstream America.

Despite his disclaimer, cynics believed that Foreman's
change of heart had as much to do with cleaning up his image
before his conspiracy trial, as it did with a shift in his philosophy. "In fact, the opposite is true," Foreman told me. "My
wife encouraged me to stay in Earth First! But by the summer
of 1990 I felt increasingly uncomfortable with the increasing
divisiveness in Earth First! and felt it was just time to get
about my own work separate from Earth First!"

Foreman explained that he still advocated judicious monkeywrenching and radical thinking. He announced plans to
start a new group to establish a nation-wide system of wilderness areas linked by roadless "green corridors," reclaimed
from over-used lands. His network would permit wild animals

to move freely from one preserve to another, encouraging cross breeding for endangered species.

He felt that Earth First! had made a serious tactical mistake in permitting unrelated political acts like flag-burning at their rallies. "I want to take the flag back," Foreman declared, "and show Americans that the people who want to preserve nature are the real patriots."

· T E N ·

ON JUNE 10, 1991, THE TRIAL of the activists whom the FBI called the "Arizona Five eco-terrorists" opened (including government plant Mike Tait, who was never put on the stand). Assistant U.S. Attorney Roslyn Moore-Silver promised the jury a case of "anarchy and revolution." Millet, Baker, and Davis faced indictments with sentences of up to thirty-five years' imprisonment and fines of up to $80,000. Foreman was dubbed "the financier, the leader, sort of the guru to get all this going." He faced a five-year prison sentence and a $10,000 fine for having donated $100 to Mark Davis to fund their "terrorism."

But the FBI was embarrassed when defense attorney Spence proved that—after the FBI had spent $2 million in an eighteen-month probe of Earth First!—*half* of all the alleged conspirators proved to be infiltrated FBI agent provocateurs!

Among the thousand hours of conversations the undercover agents had recorded was even more embarrassing evidence. Mike Tait had forgotten he was still wired when he told a fellow agent, "Foreman isn't really the guy we need to pop, I mean in terms of an actual perpetrator. This is the guy we need to pop to send a message, and that's all we're really doing."

Even worse for the FBI's case against Foreman was the

tape recorded by an FBI helicopter circling his house, which revealed that it was FBI agent Mike Tait who had urged sabotaging nuclear plants and Foreman had firmly ordered him to drop that plan. Foreman was amazed that even in his home he was being eavesdropped on and recorded by an FBI spy plane. Charges against Tait were abruptly dropped.

In view of the tapes exonerating him and incriminating the FBI, I asked Foreman how he thought the FBI had hoped to make out a case against him.

"Well, that's the question," he said, laughing. "I think it's just the vagueness of conspiracy law, and the prosecution just hoped to scare the jury and heap up so much evidence about other people that I would get smeared in the process. But they knew they had a weak case."

Other embarrassments for the FBI surfaced. Foreman's wife Nancy reported that one FBI agent had urged her to leave her husband. Another activist revealed that FBI agents had threatened to take away custody of his children if he didn't "tell all" to the FBI.

Spence accused the FBI of "selective prosecution." He pointed out that none of the right-wingers who had contributed millions illegally to the Contras in the Iran-Contra conspiracy had been prosecuted. And the pressure for an attack on nuclear plants had not come from Earth First!ers but had been deliberate provocations by the FBI spy Mike Tait. It was Tait, too, who pressed Davis to get some money from Foreman. That made the FBI guilty of entrapment.

Evidence against Millet, Baker, and Davis was given by the FBI's star witness, turncoat Ron Frazier, who was paid more than $50,000 by the FBI. He also admitted in court that if he had not been able to inform for the FBI, he had intended to "pull a Rambo" and kill participants at the 1988 Earth First! Rendezvous.

After a two-week recess, the prosecution abruptly dropped its nuclear-conspiracy case in exchange for a plea bargain to lesser charges. The five defendants decided to accept the deal rather than risk the verdict of a small-town jury. Those jurists might have proved reluctant to accept the disclosures that the FBI had been forced to invent an anti-nuclear conspiracy where none had existed.

"Accepting the plea bargain was not at my initiative," Foreman told me. "It was an extremely difficult decision for me, since most people felt I would be found not guilty. But the prosecution would not consider any plea bargains unless they were a package deal. I had to consider the others."

Mark Davis was sentenced to six years in prison. The other monkeywrenchers received sentences ranging from thirty days to three years. The prosecution was forced to drop all charges against Foreman except one. They cited him for inscribing a copy of his book *Eco-defense* for an FBI agent who had requested it, "Happy wrenching." For this "crime," incredibly, he received a sentence of five years' probation.

· ELEVEN ·

THE GOVERNMENT'S PROSECUTION of Earth First! activists failed to frighten other dedicated environmentalists from joining. By 1992 the organization had twenty thousand members in some fifty "bureaus," making it the fastest-growing environmental "direct action" group after Greenpeace.

"We represent a certain style, a particular point of view," wrote the editors of Earth First!'s journal. "And we don't plan to change." Earth First!ers continue to organize two or three environmental protests a month.

I asked Greenpeace's David McTaggart his opinion of Earth First! He told me, "I support the aim of working for a better world. Many different groups have different ways of working. Nobody can sit in judgment of whether one group or another is right in how they tackle a problem."

Foreman is now executive editor of *Wild Earth Magazine*, which supports a lot of different environment groups, and is also working on four new books. His main project is developing the Wildlands Project, a clearing house headquarters that is helping grass-roots regional groups around the country and in Canada develop a major wilderness restoration plan for North America. "We're going to try to piece that together as a continent-wide system," he told me. "We want to be a coordinating group, not a membership organization."

I asked Foreman whether his and other conservation groups would have greater difficulty in winning popular support during a recession, when many people were losing jobs.

"Well, the media likes to hype that up," he replied. "But a public opinion poll shows that the American public supports the Endangered Species Act even when it may be harmful to jobs or economic growth. And as for the Rocky Mountain states, considered to be fairly anti-environment, sixty-nine percent of the people supported the Act."

The Earth First!ers and Dave Foreman may achieve only small victories, but each victory is a setback for despoilers of the environment. News of their exploits raises the consciousness of Americans. If angry business interests see them as a wild band of "lunatics," it needs to be remembered that this was how a wild-eyed radical named John Muir was also once denounced, until he had won over enough converts to make him "respectable."

As a result of Earth First!'s extension of the parameters of political debate, the conservative environmental organizations may have become more activist to some extent.

"We allowed the mainstream groups to move a little more

in that direction," Foreman told me, "and still be perceived as moderates." Making the environment a hot issue by their activities, they aroused public sentiment. And voters put pressure on lawmakers for new, effective conservation laws.

Foreman and the Earth First!ers raised troubling questions about radical environmentalism that need to be addressed by those who care about the earth. Do acts of "civil disobedience," such as illegal confrontations in forests and deserts, further or hinder the cause of environmentalists? Has environmentalism now become such an accepted American goal that it is no longer necessary or even helpful for activists to try to force change by physical confrontation? Are job considerations, such as employment for loggers, to be given priority over the creatures who live in the forests the loggers cut down for their livelihood?

These questions may still be problems for new generations to solve as America heads into the twenty-first century.

A Short History of the Environmental Movement

· ONE ·

NORTH AMERICA'S ORIGINAL environmentalists were the Indians. They believed that man was only one of earth's many creatures, with no more special rights to the earth's riches than any other living being. Every mountain and waterfall was respected as sheltering a sacred spirit. Many tribes referred to earth as the "mother," the source of all life. To harm her would be only to harm themselves. So, though they took their living from the wilderness, they never took more than they needed and they tried not to disrupt the balance of nature.

The early American settlers had a very different view of the natural world. They saw themselves as separate from the rest of nature. It was their right, even their duty, to "civilize" the wilderness. The new land was theirs to use as profitably as they could. The vast forests of the Northeast were chopped down and turned into farmland. Animals like the beaver were hunted and trapped almost to extinction. Yet few early Americans thought about the shifts they made in the balance of nature. America was a vast territory, with seemingly limitless resources.

As more and more land in the East was settled, businesses and government enticed people to go west. Railroad companies offered idyllic pictures of fruitful farms and rising towns, hoping to increase immigrant traffic and expand their routes out west. They also offered a new "sport," shooting buffalo from train windows as the train sped over the plains. General Nelson Miles estimated that in the Arkansas River area alone, over four million buffalo were slaughtered. This destruction of the buffalo herds meant the loss of the Plains Indians' primary food source and their way of life.

Nothing sped westward expansion more than the discovery of gold in California in 1848. All through the 1850s, the gold rush brought wagon trains creaking through the Western plains. While some hopefuls made it all the way to the gold-fields, other pioneers settled on the cheap land offered along the way. With the buffalo gone, the prairies were turned over to cultivation and ranching.

A few people began to speak out for the land. The most notable was Henry David Thoreau, whose book *Walden*, published in 1864, praised a life lived in accord with nature and asserted that "In wilderness is the preservation of the world." But most people viewed the early environmentalists as enemies of progress, exasperating obstacles to the opening of the West to lumber and mining companies and ranchers for commercial exploitation.

· TWO ·

IT WASN'T UNTIL 1872 THAT environmentalists managed to persuade Congress to establish Yellowstone as a national park, making it the first protected forest area in the United States. The modern movement for conservation began one year later, when the American Association for the Advancement of Science petitioned Congress to stop the depletion of American's natural resources.

This was a time when the public was largely unaware of the ecological threats posed by overuse of America's natural resources and wilderness habitats. Western settlers, ranchers, and miners were more concerned with making a living. So were large corporations, who made the largest contributions to the campaign funds of legislators, governors, and presidents. When the handful of environmentalists and scientists prodded Congress into creating a Forestry Division in 1876, the new agency was given neither enforcement funds nor any real power.

Of those early environmentalists, none was more effective or tireless in fighting for the wilderness than naturalist John Muir. His inspiring love affair with the wilderness roused increasing numbers of Americans to demand the preservation of the nation's beautiful virgin lands. He also stirred President Theodore Roosevelt to set aside more than a million acres of timberland as national parks and preserves. Two years later, in 1905, Roosevelt created the U.S. Forestry Service to strictly regulate commercial operations in the forests.

Interest in preserving the environment grew steadily as Americans discovered the great beauty and wealth of wildlife in America's parklands. The Sierra Club, founded in 1892, enjoyed a rapid growth in membership by combining environmental legislative efforts with vacation trips to the national parks.

The National Audubon Society was formed in 1905 in response to the impending extinction of the buffalo and other wildlife. They succeeded in compelling Congress to pass the Lacy Act, the first federal legislation to protect American wildlife. When the fashion for feathered hats led to the near extinction of some bird species, they were instrumental in forcing the passage of the Migratory Bird Treaty Act of 1918 between the U.S. and Canada, which set strict limits on bird hunting.

In the 1930s the U.S. suffered an ecological disaster that made Americans look at conservation in a new way. This was a threat not to wildlife or the wilderness but to the land itself. Beginning in 1933, huge dust storms boiled over the Great Plains states, raising walls of dirt that penetrated eyes, ears, and noses. People coughed up black phlegm. Sand buried farmyards, fences, machinery, sheds, and houses. Sighed one farmer, "I'm just settin' at the window countin' the farms of Kansas as they fly by."

The prairies had been overgrazed. Trees which had held moisture in the earth had been cut and not replaced. Fields were exhausted from overcultivation. The land simply blew away, creating a huge dust bowl from South Dakota to Oklahoma. President Franklin D. Roosevelt quickly introduced conservation measures to slow down and eliminate the soil erosion. Millions of farmers and ranchers were made aware of the need for conservation as a matter of sheer survival.

· **THREE** ·

SLOWLY BUT TIRELESSLY, environmental activists were educating Americans about the importance of preserving America's natural treasures. The number and the ranks of environmental groups climbed steadily, from the Sierra Club and the Audubon Society to the Appalachian Mountain Club, the Wild Life Protection Fund, the Izaak Walton League, and the Wilderness Society.

At the close of World War II, a dangerous new pollutant arrived: the atomic bomb. Americans were at first jubilant when the U.S. dropped the bomb on Japan, bringing an end to the war in the Pacific. But the awesome spectacle of the nuclear bomb's explosive power made many Americans apprehensive, especially when it was revealed that radiation poisoning spread by the bomb's mushroom cloud had killed up to 200,000 Japanese civilians in Hiroshima and Nagasaki.

The specter of deadly radiation hit home after the war when tests of a new nuclear bomb in Nevada showered areas as far away as Troy, New York, with radioactive fallout. Not until 1997 did the government admit that almost the whole population of the country had actually received some radiation from this test. Angry citizens and environmentalists demanded a ban on all nuclear tests in the atmosphere. But it wasn't until

1963 that John F. Kennedy signed such a test ban treaty, along with Great Britain and the Soviet Union.

World War II saw another form of pollution introduced. With the threat of war in the mid-1930s, the American defense industry rapidly increased production, and their factory smokestacks filled the skies with air pollutants and carbon dioxide. This added to the pollution already produced by millions of cars on America's vast network of roads, highways, and interstates, creating the lethal combination called "smog"— polluted air that stung eyes, fouled lungs, and caused coughing fits and sometimes death.

Smog's lethal power was first felt in 1948 in Donora, Pennsylvania, where twenty people died in five days, simply from breathing the air. Smog was subsequently blamed for fully four thousand deaths in London, and two hundred in New York City.

In the affluent fifties, Americans were enjoying an increasingly high standard of living, thanks to the wonders of industry and science. Crediting big business for bettering their lives, most people paid scant attention to what the corporations were doing to the environment in the name of economic expansion.

But as awareness of the dangers of air and water pollution grew, an aroused public began to demand that something be done about it. During President Kennedy's administration in the early 1960s, public pressure forced Congress to set up no fewer than thirteen committees to study and try to solve environmental problems. In 1963, Congress passed the first Clean Air Act.

One person who profoundly changed the public's complacency about the environment was Rachel Carson. When her book *Silent Spring* first appeared in 1962, many were frightened by its portrait of the darker, unknown side of scientific progress. But her research about the harmful effects of pesticides on wildlife and humans could not be disputed. The congressional hearings that investigated Carson's allegations led to the banning of the pesticide DDT and put an end to the legal dumping of chemical wastes dangerous to humans, wildlife, and sea life. Her book also made American consumers more skeptical of the scientific advances promoted by big business, while showing how much a single informed voice could accomplish.

· FOUR ·

AMERICA'S GROWING INVOLVEMENT in the Vietnam War during the sixties and early seventies was met by stormy opposition, especially from millions of young people. They saw the government as a captive of the huge defense industry—the military-industrial complex—and of big corporations who made large donations to election campaigns and put profits before concern for the ecology. Many activists and leaders in the new environmental groups came from the anti-war movement. They adapted the tactics they had used in anti-war protests and in civil rights actions for the new war against pollution.

Young activists and citizens demonstrated across the country in support of Senator Gaylord Nelson of Wisconsin's proposal that April 22, 1970, be named the first annual Earth Day. Nelson warned, "Progress—American style—adds up each year to 200 million tons of smoke and fumes, 7 million junked cars, 20 million tons of paper, 48 million cans and 28 million bottles."

More than 20 million Americans and an estimated 80 million people abroad participated in the rallies and protests, making this the largest global demonstration in history. The protests took many forms. College students plugged polluting sewage pipes with cement. Volunteers cleaned up littered ghettos and beaches. Car engines were buried as polluters in mock funerals. Large corporations were directly confronted with their crimes against the environment. For example, large piles of empty Coke cans were dumped on the lawn of the Coca Cola company's headquarters to protest the company's failure to recycle cans.

One hundred years after environmentalists had won the first small concessions from the government, environmentalism had become a cause that almost all Americans could support. The government responded to the public's enthusiasm and environmentalists' pressure by passing a new Clean Air Act and a Toxic Substances Control Act. They also created the Environmental Protection Agency (EPA), an organization with the power and funding to take action against the full range of environmental threats.

The seventies offered no end of ecological disasters for environmentalists and the new watchdog agency to combat. Between 1973 and 1977, tankers poured millions of gallons of oil into the oceans in over five thousand spills, fouling beaches and killing seabirds and animals. The problem of smog in major cities grew worse and worse. New nuclear plants opened, increasing the chances of catastrophic nuclear leaks and worsening the problem of nuclear waste disposal. Forests dwindled, while deserts grew. The extent of pollution in our waterways was demonstrated when Lake Erie, one of the Great Lakes, was declared a dead lake because it was so full of industrial waste. So was the Cuyahoga River, which actually caught on fire.

But, as the first Earth Day had demonstrated, ecology was now a global issue. Pollution did not respect national borders, and what appeared to be a local problem could have global consequences.

One such international problem was the "greenhouse effect," which was first realized in 1967. Scientists warned that the increased amount of atmospheric carbon dioxide—which is contained in car exhaust and released by burning fossil fuels like coal and oil—was making the earth act like a florist's greenhouse. They speculated that world temperatures would rise increasingly, changing global weather patterns and causing a possible Arctic meltdown.

Other "greenhouse" gases were identified as chlorofluorocarbons (CFCs)—released by spray cans and refrigeration units—and related gases. Environmentalists succeeded in getting Congress to pass acts restricting use of these gases, but many other countries continued to use them.

David McTaggart recognized the global nature of pollution and formed Greenpeace in 1971 to fight threats to the health of the seas and its creatures. From its first four-man protest, Greenpeace would grow to be the world's largest international environmental group, with headquarters in eleven countries.

In 1972, the United States joined the United Nations in recognizing that the survival of everyone depended on maintaining the earth's health. The UN called for international cooperation to achieve that goal in the Conference on the Human Environment held in Stockholm, Sweden.

The late 1970s saw two new threats to global ecology. Scientists warned that CFCs, the same chemicals that contributed to the greenhouse effect, were also destroying the ozone layer. That layer screened out most of the sun's dangerous ultraviolet radiation, protection that was vital to human health and the survival of plant life. A huge hole in the ozone layer had already appeared over Antarctica, causing an increase in the cases of skin cancer in the southern hemisphere.

Acid rain and snow, caused by the sulphur dioxide and hydrogen chloride emissions from coal-burning factories, were also destroying life in hundreds of rivers and lakes in America and around the world. A study in 1977 found that fully 95 percent of U.S. river basins were polluted. Oceanographer Jacques Cousteau, working for the UN, reported similarly bleak findings from his study of the Mediterranean.

"On earth is only one body of water, which is constantly traveling from one river to one lake to one ocean," he wrote. "The way the moving ocean is exploited and polluted is no longer a matter of 'internal affairs,' since it may severely affect other nations, now and for generations to come. . . . Governments, spurred by their citizens, must develop policies to halt these practices."

Toward the end of the seventies, two incidents drove home how devastating environmental catastrophes could be. Citizens of Love Canal in Niagara Falls, New York, became highly concerned at how many of them suffered from birth defects, and cancer, miscarriages, epilepsy, liver disease, and other illnesses. What had made them so sick?

When the New York State Health Department investigated, they found that the neighborhood had been built on land that contained fifteen chemical waste dumps of the Hooker Chemical Company. Some eighty thousand tons of chemicals, including deadly dioxin, were leaching into their homes, schools, playgrounds, and drinking wells. In 1978, President Jimmy Carter declared Love Canal a federal emergency. All the residents were evacuated and their houses were boarded up. The Canal is still largely a ghost town.

The cost of cleaning up Hooker's waste dumps would have been astronomical—and this was just one of 838 similar chemical dumps that the EPA estimated existed in the U.S. Congress responded by creating a superfund to handle future clean-ups.

One year later, an event occurred that could have been even more disastrous than Love Canal. At the Three Mile Island nuclear plant near Middletown, Pennsylvania, radioactive gases escaped through the venting system. The plant, on a runaway course to a catastrophic meltdown, was brought under control just in the nick of time.

How dangerous the Three Mile Island disaster could have been was shown seven years later in the USSR, when a reactor in the nuclear power plant in Chernobyl exploded. Thirty-one people died from radiation burns, and thousands more had their lives shortened by the long-term effects of radiation poisoning. Food was contaminated all across northern Europe. Hundreds of square miles in the Soviet Union were evacuated and permanently closed to rehabitation. After the Chernobyl disaster, the cry for stricter controls over building and operating nuclear reactors became worldwide.

· **FIVE** ·

JIMMY CARTER WAS THE FIRST president to support environmentalism actively since Theodore Roosevelt. His administration issued a *Global 2000 Report* which forecast that by the new millennium, the earth would be "more crowded, more polluted, less stable ecologically." It predicted famine in Africa, skyrocketing food and fuel prices, and the disappearance of one fifth of all species on earth due to destruction of the rainforests. By 1997 famine in Africa had come to pass, as well as famine in North Korea, while food and fuel prices did rise considerably, even in the United States.

But despite Carter's good intentions, very little positive

action for the environment was undertaken. While the public had become much more aware and supportive of environmental causes, environmental groups and lobbyists working in Washington were winning fewer victories, and becoming far more accepting of compromises with the powerful timber, mining, and ranching industries.

Environmental lobbyist Dave Foreman became disillusioned with the world of Washington bureaucracy and turned to direct action to save wilderness areas. In June 1981, he and three others formed Earth First!, a group that physically confronted loggers, using their bodies to protect the forests and wilderness areas threatened by big business interests.

The conservative backlash against environmentalists that Dave Foreman feared arrived in full force under the administration of Ronald Reagan, who named James Watt as his Secretary of the Interior. Vehemently pro-business, Watt issued permits for mining in one of the oldest and largest wilderness areas. He even tried to allow oil drilling along California's coastline, which had already suffered repeatedly from oil tanker spills.

With the Sierra Club leading the fight, and much of the public incensed over Watt's opening of protected wilderness, Watt was forced to resign. Margaret Thatcher, England's Prime Minister, later adopted Watt's philosophy, calling environmentalists "the enemy within." But in 1988, because of public pressure, she had to reverse herself, and now called protection of the environment "one of the greatest challenges of the late twentieth century."

One sign of hope for environmentalists in the nineties was the 1987 agreement by thirteen industrial nations, including the United States, to ban the use of chlorofluorocarbons by the year 2000. As the new millennium approached, people all around the world were joining to press for conservation measures to protect earth's natural resources.

At the 1997 White House Conference on Climate Change, President Bill Clinton declared that the United States "must show leadership" on global warming and "do the responsible thing . . . to avoid leaving our children and grandchildren with a catastrophe."

At an international conference in Kyoto, Japan, in December 1997, world leaders signed a treaty to limit the production of the carbon dioxide gases causing the global warming responsible for catastrophic drought, floods, rising seas, excessive rainfall, and upsets to agricultural production. President Clinton declared the United States would sign if special concessions were made. But United States manufacturing interests opposed the treaty as injurious to their profits, and United States labor unions threatened that it would cost hundreds of thousands of United States jobs. Accordingly, the Senate was prepared to reject the treaty even if the president signed it.

In the United States, nationwide polls conducted by the *Wall Street Journal* and NBC showed that four out of five Americans now supported measures to protect the environment. "Environmentalism has become an issue like motherhood and apple pie," declared Peter Dykstra of Greenpeace. "No one wants to be seen as anti-environmental."

In the past hundred years, the environmental movement has gone through a sea change. Starting with a handful of people who were considered "nature nuts," it has won the support of the vast majority of Americans and grown to encompass hundreds of organizations.

(S. C. Delaney/U. S. EPA)

The Fight to Save the Earth Today and Tomorrow

"THIS COUNTRY," DECLARED Michael Deland, chairman of the White House Council on Environmental Quality, "is the most wasteful on the face of this earth. With only 5 percent of the earth's population, we use 26 percent of the world's oil; produce 290 million tons of toxic waste; and overload the atmosphere with 22 percent of the world's dioxide emissions."

Our government itself has been one of the worst offenders on this count. Each year, for example, three million federal workers have thrown out over 270,000 tons of paper, which required the cutting of almost five million trees. The amount of energy used to operate government facilities each year could heat and light every American home for forty days.

This situation improved considerably in 1995 when a new Congress and President Bill Clinton "downsized" the government, dramatically reducing the number of federal employees.

At the same time, however, the Defense Department's budget was fattened by $26 billion. The Pentagon's maintenance of its huge fleet of trucks, ships, and aircraft continues to pollute the earth with over 400,000 tons of toxic sludge, solvents, acids, and heavy metals every year.

America's citizens are also part of the problem. Each year the average American uses thirty-seven thousand gallons of water and three hundred gallons of gasoline, and throws away eighty-four pounds of plastic. Plastics make up 30 percent of our garbage and take hundreds of years to degrade. We are rapidly running out of garbage dumps, and the ones we have are overflowing.

Americans need to reexamine how we are part of the ecological problem and what we can do to become part of the solution. As Vice President Al Gore said in 1995, "We need to recognize that we have a responsibility as stewards of the

Earth. . . . We have to change our way of thinking and recognize that we are connected to the Earth. . . . We have to look beyond ourselves and recognize the effect of our actions today on our children and grandchildren tomorrow."

What has happened to the environmental causes fought for so courageously by Muir, Carson, McTaggart, and Foreman? What must be done to continue their struggles and to cope with new environmental problems which have arisen?

· TWO ·

DESPITE MUIR'S WARNINGS about the dangers of deforestation, the United States cuts more trees annually than any other country in the world. Where once 25 million acres of forest covered western Washington and Oregon, now only 3.4 million acres remain. The Wilderness Society estimates that if logging continues at the present rate, *all* unprotected old-growth trees in these states will be gone in less than twenty years.

Conservationists have won some victories for the forests. Our government now compels lumber companies to replant trees where they have cut old growth. In 1992, restrictions were also placed on logging in many old-growth forests, including seven million acres which are the habitat of endangered wildlife such as the northern spotted owl.

Activists in Greenpeace and Earth First! continue to put their lives on the line to protect the environment. In a typical protest action in California, Earth First! protesters dressed in camouflage and ran into the woods next to falling trees, compelling the loggers to stop cutting for fear of killing them.

One hopeful sign, reported by the American Paper Institute, is that Americans are recycling more paper than ever before. Paper recycling drives by schools and towns have been so successful that the price paid for paper to be recycled has soared, making recycling profitable as well as ecologically beneficial. And recycling paper saves more than trees. It uses half the energy and water for every ton of paper made, creates 35 percent less water pollution, reduces the garbage in our dumps, and decreases acid rain, since the paper industry is the single largest user of fossil oil fuel in the world.

The fight begun by John Muir to preserve the American wilderness has had mixed results in our time. His warning against the over-building of Western dams has been largely ignored, resulting in the disappearance of salmon from California rivers. Some power companies have been forced to put "fish ladders" in the dams to enable the salmon to swim upstream to spawning grounds, but the effort has not been successful.

Western senators have also swept aside Muir's opposition to allowing grazing in many wilderness areas. As a result, 20 million acres have been overgrazed and are threatened by erosion. So far, ranchers have been able to block the Interior Department's efforts to reduce this overuse by raising fees for grazing cattle on public grasslands.

On the positive side, Congress passed the California Desert Protection Act in 1994, which set aside almost 10 million acres of desert as national parkland and preserves, creating the largest wilderness area outside Alaska.

The battle for forests and wilderness is now fought on a global scale, with world attention focused on saving tropical rain forests in Asia and South America. Each year the earth loses about 42 million acres of rain forest to lumbering, mining, and agriculture. Scientists worry that massive rain forest destruction could bring about dangerous changes in the global climate. With these forests we will also lose up to a fifth of all plant and animal species, including rare plants that provide important medicines.

"Forests provide far more than economic products and recreations," Eric Eckholm of Worldwatch Institute points out. "They assist in the global cycling of water, oxygen, carbon and nitrogen. They lend stability to hydrological systems, reducing the severity of floods. . . . Trees keep soil from washing off . . . [and] sediment out of rivers and reservoirs. . . . Forests house millions of plant and animal species that will disappear if woodlands are destroyed."

While Muir was ridiculed for promoting the concept of animal rights and the need to protect the habitats of endangered species, today millions of environmentalists and animal-rights advocates fight to preserve wildlife on land and in the seas.

Successful battles have been fought to save habitats of animals such as the northern spotted owl. Other species have been reintroduced into areas where they once thrived. For example, after a fourteen-year fight to restore the ecological balance of Yellowstone and Idaho, gray wolves were brought back into the region. Hope has been given in the fight to save the African elephant from extinction, by the international ban on traffic in elephant ivory; poachers in Africa, however, remain a problem.

Environmentalists have continued fighting to preserve old-growth forests, habitats for hundreds of creatures. In November 1996, nine Earth First! and other environmentalists, including actor Woody Harrelson, climbed up the cables of the Golden Gate Bridge in San Francisco with signs and banners, causing a six-hour traffic snarl, to denounce excess logging in Northern California. All were arrested.

Constant protests and demonstrations by Earth First!, Greenpeace and other environmentalists have succeeded in saving the habitats of many endangered species. Of those on the first list of endangered species, only a few have actually fallen extinct; the rest remain viable in the wild—a spectacular achievement, considering that the first list included dozens of species thought beyond hope. Many creatures once described as doomed, including the bald eagle, peregrine falcon, marbled murrelet, northern spotted owl, and gray whale, have been removed from the priority protection list.

Despite these successes, millions of species are still in danger of extinction from habitat destruction and hunting. The International Council on Bird Preservation warns that over one thousand of the nine thousand species of birds in the world are threatened or endangered today. But the United States includes only forty of these on the endangered species list that protects the animals against hunting and the destruction of their habitats.

· THREE ·

RACHEL CARSON'S CRUSADE TO keep pesticides and other pollutants out of our air and water is continued by American consumers who have become more savvy about the agricultural industry. A recent Harris Poll found that 81 percent of consumers consider organically grown food safer, though it is more expensive, and the number of organic farms has grown considerably. The U.S. Department of Agriculture has also turned to organic farms for more of the foods it provides for school lunches.

But the pace of change is agonizingly slow. In 1974, ten years after the publication of *Silent Spring*, Congress required the EPA to review all pesticides and determine which ones should be removed from the market. Today only thirty out of the six hundred pesticides available have been tested. The untested chemicals are still on sale. "At this rate," said Jim Aidala, a one-time congressional pesticide expert, "the review of existing pesticides will be completed in the year 15,000."

Meanwhile, the EPA has found that almost 40 percent of river miles are too polluted to permit swimming, drinking, or fishing. Most of this pollution is caused by pesticide-tainted agricultural runoff.

Agricultural runoff, along with the illegal dumping of sewage and industrial waste, has also contributed to the poisoning of the oceans. But environmentalists—some coming from unlikely places—are trying to reduce this pollution through the courts. David Satlman, director of the Surfrider Foundation, has declared, "Surfers are environmentalists whether they like it or not." His organization successfully charged two pulp mills with dumping toxic chemicals on the beaches where they surfed. The companies were forced to pay a fine of over $5.7 million and to spend $50 million cleaning up the waste. If more such court actions are brought, polluting can be made simply too expensive for anti-environmental companies.

Air pollution, caused primarily by car exhaust, power-generating plants, and factories, is still a serious problem in this country. The introduction of unleaded gasoline has helped reduce toxic car exhaust; so have catalytic converters, which cut down on nitrogen oxide exhausts, and are now required by many states. Communities have also tried to cut down on the number of cars on the road by promoting car pools, mass transit, and biking. Some companies have introduced "telecommuting," allowing members of their staff to stay at home and communicate with the office by computer link.

Power plants produce 20 million tons of sulfur dioxide a year, along with other toxic chemicals. The EPA has attempted to get companies to switch to low-sulfur coal or oil, or natural gas, with some success. The pollutants reported released in 1993 (the latest reported statistics) had decreased 12.6 percent from the 1992 figure. Putting scrubbers on

smokestacks would also reduce the pollutants, but many companies claim these are too expensive to install and maintain.

The one sure way to reduce power plant pollution would
be to reduce our use of electric power. Environmentalists, the
government, and electric companies are all working to get
consumers to use electricity as sparingly and efficiently as
possible.

Power plants and industrial smokestacks are also primary
contributors to the global problems of acid rain, the greenhouse effect, and the depletion of the ozone layer.

Largely because of the failure of countries other than the
U.S. to cut back on pollutants, the hole in the ozone layer has
continued to grow since its discovery in 1985. The hole now
covers an area three times larger than the continental United
States.

What of David McTaggart's crusade to stop nuclear pollution of the air and sea? With the single exception of the world-
condemned French atomic tests in 1995, the earth has
remained free of the danger of atmospheric nuclear tests. The
major nuclear powers—the United States, Russia, Great
Britain, and finally France—signed a Nuclear Test Ban Treaty
in 1963. The United Nations has been keeping a wary eye on
North Korea, which was reported to be developing nuclear
weapons.

The disposal of nuclear wastes, which emit high levels of
radiation for thousands of years, remains a serious problem.
Under its new leadership, Greenpeace continues to stage actions against the transportation and ocean dumping of such
wastes. If Greenpeace's fight needed any justification, it was
provided in April 1993, when a tank of nuclear waste exploded in Tomsk, Russia, the worst nuclear accident since
Chernobyl. A radioactive cloud moved across Siberia, narrowly missing irradiating half a million people.

In the United States, most nuclear wastes are stored at 108 sites in the thirty-three states that generated them, pending some long-term plan for handling them. Even these facilities are not completely safe. There is always the danger that the waste piles will explode, spreading radioactive material over thousands of miles. Ocean dumping is also unsafe, since no container can resist eroding and leaking in the waters over the centuries. So the problem of nuclear waste disposal remains. Meanwhile, the stockpiles continue to grow.

In nuclear power plants, disasters and near-disasters continue to occur. For ten years, Maine environmentalists had been trying to close the Maine Yankee nuclear power plant as a public danger. Then in 1991, fire broke out at the plant, forcing a shutdown until new safety measures could be introduced.

The safety of nuclear plants came into further question when Ralph Nader's Public Citizen Committee revealed in 1992 that there had been 350 violations of security measures at U.S. plants. Because of vociferous environmental opposition, the building of new nuclear plants has slowed, the number of those operating declining from 111 in 1991 to 109 in 1992, with no further building through 1994.

· FIVE ·

WHAT CAN INDIVIDUALS DO TO continue the fight waged by Muir, Carson, McTaggart, and Foreman to save the environment?

Many of us are familiar with ways we can reduce our own consumption of natural resources. We can conserve energy, and thus reduce the damage done by energy-creating fuels. For example, we can lower the thermostat in cold weather and wear sweaters. We can switch to energy-conserving neon bulbs and tubes and turn off lights when we leave a room. We can recycle paper, aluminum cans, and motor oil, and reuse bottles, containers, and shopping bags. We can walk or ride bikes as much as possible.

When something tears, wears, or breaks, we can repair it if possible instead of throwing it out and replacing it. We can use energy-saving appliances. We can reduce water usage by installing water-conserving shower heads and placing bricks in the toilet tank.

"We should cut U.S. consumption of energy, petroleum products, water, beef, wood, paper, and minerals in half during the next decade," Dave Foreman proposes. "We should recycle virtually everything. . . . Pay our rent for living on this beautiful, blue-green living earth."

You can keep up with what's happening on the environmental front and what you can do to help by following the news on TV or in the papers, or watching the new twenty-four-hour Ecology Channel on cable TV.

Be aware of upcoming legislation affecting the environment and let your representatives—from the local to the national level—know where you stand.

But helping to get needed legislation passed is only half the job. The other half is making sure the laws are strictly enforced by well-funded and well-staffed regulatory agencies, agencies that have the independence and authority to act as our environmental police.

A perfect day to begin participating in environmental activities and demonstrations in your community is April 22: Earth Day. Earth Day celebrations offer the opportunity to join an environmental group in your neighborhood and to meet other activists who share your concerns about our planet. There is a list of national organizations you can join or get information from on the following pages.

Our world is like a living organism, with all its resources playing a part in the larger world's health. You can imagine the forests acting like lungs, supplying life-giving oxygen. Rivers, lakes, and oceans are as vital as the circulatory system which brings blood to all the body's organs. The ozone layer offers protection to the whole earth, like a surrounding layer of skin. If harm comes to any of these parts, the whole planet's health suffers.

This is the only earth we have. If it were not for the courageous and persistent struggles of environmental pioneers and their successors, the planet would be in far greater trouble than it is today. We owe them our gratitude.

But more than that, we need to continue their fight—to save our earth in the twenty-first century.

And the time to start is now.

ENVIRONMENTAL ORGANIZATIONS YOU CAN JOIN

American Shore and Beach Preservation Association, P. O. Box 279, Middleton, CA 95461. (900 members)

Animal Protection Institute of America, 2831 Fruitridge Rd., Sacramento, CA 95822. (75,000 members)

Appalachian Mountain Club, 5 Joy St., Boston, MA 02108. (54,952 members)

Center for Marine Conservation, 1725 De Sales St. NW, Washington, DC 20036.

Coalition on the Environment & Jewish Life, 443 Park Ave. South, 11th Floor, New York, NY 10016-7322.

Common Cause, 2030 M St. NW, Washington, DC 20036.

Consumers Union of the U.S., 101 Truman Ave., Yonkers, NY 10703. (405,990 members)

Defenders of Wildlife, 1244 19th St. NW, Washington, DC 20036. (80,000 members)

Earth First!, P. O. Box 5871, Tucson, AZ 85703.

EarthSave, 706 Frederick St., Santa Cruz, CA 95062.

Greenpeace Foundation, 1436 U St. NW, Washington, DC 20009. (2.9 million members)

International Association of Educators for World Peace, P.O. Box 3282, Mastin Lake Station, Huntsville, AL 35810. (25,000 members)

National Audubon Society, 700 Broadway, New York, NY 10003. (538,151 members)

National Environmental Health Association, 720 S. Colorado Blvd., Suite 970, Denver, CO 80222. (5,500 members)

National Wildlife Federation, 1400 16th St. NW, Washington, DC 20036-2266. (4.7 million members)

Nature Conservancy, 1815 N. Lyon St., Arlington, VA 22202. (692,000 members)

The Naturist Society, 454 Main St., Oshkosh, WI 54901. (20,000 members)

People for the Ethical Treatment of Animals, P.O. Box 45216, Washington, DC 20015. (500,000 members)

Rainforest Futures, 518 Meder St., Santa Cruz, CA 95060.

Save Our Shores, 2222 E. Cliff Drive, Santa Cruz, CA 95061.

Sierra Club, 730 Polk St., San Francisco, CA 94109 (564,360 members)

Soil and Water Conservation Society of America, 7515 N.E. Ankeny Rd., Ankeny, IA 50021-9764.

Thoreau Society, 156 Belknap St., Concord, MA 01742. (1,500 members)

UN Environment Program, 2 United Nations Plaza, Rm. 1812, New York, NY 10017.

Water Pollution Control Federation, 601 Wythe St., Alexandria, VA 22314-1994. (32,000 members)

Wilderness Society, 900 17th St. NW, Washington, DC 20006. (271,268 members)

The Wildlands Project, 1955 W. Grant Road, Suite 148A, Tucson, AZ 85745.

World Future Society, 7910 Woodmont Ave., Suite 450, Washington, DC 20814. (30,000 members)

World Wildlife Fund, 1250 24th St. NW, Washington, DC 20037. (1.25 million members)

Zero Population Growth, 1400 16th St. NW, Washington, DC 20036. (50,000 members)

BIBLIOGRAPHY AND
SUGGESTED FURTHER READING

(recommended reading indicated by *)

Bade, William Frederic. *The Life and Letters of John Muir*. 2 volumes. Boston: Houghton Mifflin, 1923, 1924.

* Brooks, Paul. *The House of Life: Rachel Carson at Work*. Boston: Houghton Mifflin, 1972.

* Brower, David. *For Earth's Sake*. Salt Lake City: Gibbs-Smith, 1990.

* ———, editor. *The Sierra Club Wilderness Handbook*. New York: Ballantine Books, 1967.

* Carson, Rachel. *The Edge of the Sea*. New York: New American Library, 1959.

* ———. *The Sea Around Us*. Revised edition. New York: New American Library, 1961.

* ———. *Silent Spring*. Greenwich, Conn.: Fawcett Publications, 1964.

* ———. *Under the Sea Wind*. New York: Simon & Schuster, 1941.

Cohen, Michael P. *The Pathless Way: John Muir and the American Wilderness*. Madison: University of Wisconsin Press, 1984.

Congressional Committee Hearings. *Coordination of Activities to the Use of Pesticides, May & June 1963 . . . on Bills for Pesticide Research and Controls, June 6, 1963*. Washington, D.C.: U.S. Government Printing Office, 1964, 1965.

Courrier, Kathleen, editor. *Life After '80: Environmental Choices We Can Live With*. Andover, Mass.: Brick House Publishing Company, 1980.

* Douglas, William O. *Muir of the Mountains*. Boston: Houghton Mifflin, 1961.

Engberg, Robert. *John Muir Summering in the Sierra*. Madison: University of Wisconsin Press, 1984.

* ———, editor. *John Muir to Yosemite & Beyond: Writings from the Years 1863–1875*. Madison: University of Wisconsin Press, 1980.

* Foreman, Dave. *Confessions of an Eco-Warrior*. New York: Harmony Books, 1991.

Fox, Stephen. *The American Conservation Movement: John Muir and His Legacy*. Madison: University of Wisconsin Press, 1985.

———. *John Muir and His Legacy*. Boston: Little, Brown & Company, 1981.

Frome, Michael. *Conscience of a Conservationist*. Knoxville: University of Tennessee Press, 1989.

* Gartner, Carol B. *Rachel Carson*. New York: Frederick Ungar Publishing Company, 1983.

* Gore, Al. *Earth in the Balance*. Boston: Houghton Mifflin, 1992.

* Harlan, Judith. *Sounding the Alarm: A Biography of Rachel Carson*. Minneapolis: Dillon Press, 1989.

Kudlinski, Kathleen V. *Rachel Carson: Pioneer of Ecology*. New York: Viking Penguin, 1988.

Latham, Jean Lee. *Rachel Carson: Who Loved the Sea*. Champaign, Ill.: Garrard Publishing Company, 1973.

Lyman, Francesca, with Irving Mintzer, Kathleen Courrier, and James MacKenzie. *The Greenhouse Trap*. Boston: Beacon Press, 1990.

* Marco, Gino J., Robert M. Hollingsworth, and William Durham, editors. *Silent Spring Revisited*. Washington, D.C.: American Chemical Society, 1987.

McClure, Matthew, editor. *SHUTDOWN: Nuclear Power on Trial*. Summertown, Tennessee: The Book Publishing Company, 1979.

Mitchell, Lee Clark. *Witnesses to a Vanishing America*. Princeton, N.J.: Princeton University Press, 1981.

* Muir, John. *The Mountains of California*. New York: The Century Company, 1911.

* ———. *My First Summer in the Sierras*. Boston: Houghton Mifflin, 1911.

———. *Northwest Passages*. Palo Alto, Calif.: Tioga Publishing Company, 1988.

———. *Our National Parks*. Boston: Houghton Mifflin, 1911.

* ———. *Stickeen*. Boston: Houghton Mifflin, 1913.

* ———. *The Story of My Boyhood and Youth*. Boston: Houghton Mifflin, 1912.

* ———. *Travels in Alaska*. Boston: Houghton Mifflin, 1915.

* Norman, Charles. *John Muir: Father of Our National Parks*. New York: Julian Messner, 1957.

Osborn, Fairfield. *Our Plundered Planet*. Boston: Little, Brown & Company, 1968.

Pell, Clairborne, and H. I. Goodwin. *Challenge of the Seven Seas*. New York: William Morrow and Company, 1966.

* Rifkin, Jeremy, and Carol Rifkin. *Voting Green*. New York: Doubleday & Co., 1992.

* Robie, David. *Eyes of Fire: Last Voyage of the Rainbow Warrior*. Philadelphia: New Society Publishers, 1987.

* Sargent, Shirley. *John Muir in Yosemite*. Yosemite, Calif.: Flying Spur Press, 1971.

* Sterling, Philip. *Sea and Earth: The Life of Rachel Carson*. New York: Thomas Y. Crowell Company, 1970.

* Sunday Times Insight Team. *Rainbow Warrior*. London, Melbourne, Auckland: London Sunday Times, 1986.

* Teale, Edwin Way. *The Wilderness World of John Muir*. Boston: Houghton Mifflin, 1954.

Udall, Stewart L. *The Quiet Crisis*. New York: Holt, Rinehart & Winston, 1963.

Whorton, James. *Before Silent Spring: Pesticides and Public Health in Pre-DDT America*. Princeton, N.J.: Princeton University Press, 1974.

* Wolfe, Linnie Marsh. *Son of the Wilderness*. New York: Alfred A. Knopf, 1945.

Young, S. Hall. *Alaska Days with John Muir*. Philadelphia: Ayer Co. Publications, 1915.

Also consulted were P.B.S. TV documentaries, and articles in and news from: *ACLU; Alternatives; American Forests; American Historical Review; American History Illustrated; The Associated Press; Audubon; Audubon Activist; Backpacker; Bulletin of the Atomic Scientists; California; Common Ground; Earth; Earth First!; Earthwatch; Eco Source; Environment; The Environmental Journal; Environs; Esquire; Focus; Fortune; Greenpeace Action; Greenpeace Magazine; Harper's Magazine; House Beautiful; Insight; In These Times; Journal of American History; Lahaina [Maui] News; Library Journal; Living Wilderness; Los Angeles Daily News; MacLean's; McClatchy News Service; Modern Maturity; The Monthly Planet; Mother Earth News; Mother Jones; The Nation; National Geographic; National Parks; National Wildlife; Nature Conservancy; New Statesman; Newsweek; The New Yorker; The New York Times; The New York Times Book Review; Oceans; Omni; Ottawa News Service; Outdoor Life; People Today; People Weekly; The Progressive; San Francisco Chronicle; Santa Cruz Sentinel; Saturday Review; Scholastic Update; Science; Science Digest; Sierra; Smithsonian; Sports Illustrated; South Maui Times; Sunset Magazine; Technology Review; Time; Universal Press Syndicate; USA Today; USA Weekend; U.S. News and World Report; Utne Reader; The Ventana; Wall Street Journal; Whole Earth Review; Wilderness Society; Wilderness Winter; World Press Review; Yankee.*

Interviews were held with David McTaggart, founder of Greenpeace; Dave Foreman, former leader of Earth First!; and Dan Haifley, leader of Save Our Shores.

INDEX

Lacoste, Pierre, 119
Lacy Act, 164
Lake Erie, 168
Lancaster, Doyle, 153
Lange, (prime minister of New
    Zealand), 118
Lindsay, John V., 81
Locksley Hall, 53–54
logging, 19–20, 25, 27, 30, 31–32,
    33, 140, 146–47, 153, 177,
    178
London, 100, 108, 166
London Dumping Convention, 112
Lornie, Mary, 100, 102–4
Love Canal, 170–71

Mafart, Alain, 117, 119–20
Maine, 110, 183
Marine Corps, 129–30
Marshall Islands, 113–14
McKay, Douglas, 75
McTaggart, David, ix, 86–125, 133,
    157–58, 169, 177, 182–83; youth,
    89; manages ski resort, 89–90;
    plans to block Mururoa nuclear
    tests by French, 88–89; in New
    Zealand; prevented from sailing,
    92–93; sailing to Mururoa, 93; en-
    dangered by French Navy, 93–96;
    compromised by French admiral,
    98–99; begins Greenpeace Europe,
    100; sails again to Mururoa to stop
    tests, 100–101; injured by French
    sailors, 102–4; sues French Navy,
    104; buys *Rainbow Warrior*, 107;
    fights ocean dumping of radioactive
    wastes, 107, 112; captured by
    Spain, 110; ridicules Secretary of
    the Interior Watts, 113; helps move
    Rongelap islanders, 113–4; French
    secretly sink the *Warrior*, 114–17;
    attempts to expose French Navy,
    117–20; retires, 123
McTaggart, Drew, 103–4
Mediterranean, 121, 170

Migratory Bird Treaty Act, 164
military-industrial complex, 167
Millet, Peg, 151–52, 155–56
Mitterand, François, 117–20
moderate conservationists, 131–32,
    135, 136, 148, 159
The Monkey Wrench Gang, 134–37
monkeywrenching, 136, 142–43, 145,
    147–48, 151–52, 154, 157
Montana, 89, 142–43
Mountains of California, 33
Muir, Anna Wanda, 28–29
Muir, Daniel, 7, 10–11, 14, 29
Muir, David, 7, 15, 19
Muir, Helen, 29, 41
Muir, John, ix, 2, 5–45, 84, 136, 139,
    158, 164, 177–79, 183; boyhood in
    Scotland, 7; brutalized by father,
    8–11; invents gadgets, 10–12; in-
    fluenced by Jeanne Carr, 12;
    breaks with father, 14; as wander-
    ing botanist, 14–15; heads for
    Yosemite, 16; as shepherd, 17;
    publishes glacier theory, 17, 19;
    operates sawmill, 20; serves as
    Yosemite guide, 20–22; with Ralph
    Waldo Emerson, 13, 22; in earth-
    quake, 23; writes for *Overland
    Monthly*, 24; explores wilderness,
    25; saves expedition members,
    25–26; marries Louise Wanda
    Strentzel, 26–27; explores Alaskan
    glaciers, 5–7, 27–28; takes wife on
    Yosemite trip, 28–29; father dies,
    29; lobbies to create Yosemite Na-
    tional Park, 30–31; on Muir Glac-
    ier, 31; attacked by enemies,
    31–32; helps organize Sierra Club,
    32; persuades Theodore Roosevelt
    of need for conservation, 33;
    clashes with Gifford Pinchot,
    33–34; takes world trip, 34; battles
    corporations, 35; joins Harriman
    expedition, 35; awarded honorary
    degrees, 36; criticizes Sierra Club,

United States (*cont.*)
121–24, 164–65, 169–73, 176–77,
180, 182–83
United States Atomic Energy Com-
mission, 113
United States Bureau of Fisheries, 56,
58, 62–63
United States Bureau of Forestry, 37
Unites States Bureau of Land Man-
agement (BLM), 134
United States Department of Agricul-
ture, 80, 82, 180
United States Department of Defense,
176
United States Department of Health,
Education and Welfare, 83
United States Department of the Inte-
rior, 82–83, 134, 178
United States Fish and Wildlife Ser-
vice, 59, 63, 65–68, 72, 75, 83
United States Forestry Division,
163
United States Forestry Service, 33,
40, 130–32, 140–41, 146–47, 150,
164
University of New Mexico, 129–30
University of Wisconsin, 12–13, 35
Utah, 137

Vancouver, 88–89, 92, 99, 104–5
van Loon, Hendrik, 61
Vega, 88–90, 92–105, 118
Vietnam War, 129–30, 146, 151, 167

Walden, 163
Wall Street Journal, 173
Washington, D.C., 130–33, 172
Washington State, 139–40, 151, 177
Watt, James, 113, 137, 139–40, 172
West Southport, Me., 73–74, 76, 78
whales, ix, 105–6, 108–11, 124

White House Conference on Climate
Control, 173
White House Council on Environmen-
tal Quality, 176
Whitney, Joseph D., 19
Wilcox, Peter, 110, 114–16, 122
Wild Earth Magazine, 158
wilderness preservation, 128, 130–31,
135–37, 139–40, 143–45, 154,
158, 164, 172, 178
Wilderness Society, 128, 130–35,
165, 177
Wildlands Project, 158
Wild Life Protection Funds, 165
Wilkinson, Peter, 107
Williamette Industries, 146–47
Williamette National Forest, 146–47
Wilson, Woodrow, 42
Wolke, Howie, 135–37, 139, 144–45,
148
women in science, 54, 56–57, 58, 59,
66, 72
Woods Hole Marine Biological Labo-
ratory, 55–56
World War I, 51
World War II, 62–63, 92, 165–66
Wyoming, 135, 140, 144, 152

Yankee nuclear power plant, 183
Yellowstone, 24, 126, 144, 179
Yosemite, ix, 14, 16–25, 28, 30–32,
35, 37–38, 40–42
The Yosemite, 42
Yosemite State and Turnpike Com-
pany, 31
Young Americans for Freedom,
129–30
Yuba River Valley, 25

Zodiacs, 94, 97, 101–3, 105–8, 112,
117, 122